The No-Nonsense Church

Essential Characteristics
of the Body of Christ

Craig DuBois

xulon
PRESS

I dedicate this book to my wife, Kathy.
*Without **you**, this book would not have been possible.*
In spite of my endless two year fixation on this project,
you constantly encouraged me to keep on writing.
Thank you for the endless confidence you express in my abilities
and for your undying faithfulness.

Acknowledgements

I would like to express my sincere gratitude to John and Jil Airhart, very dear friends, whose generosity, support, and encouragement has made this publication possible. May God bless them abundantly in Christ. I would also like to thank those parishioners that I have served throughout the years who have encouraged me in my teachings and pastoral ministry. Most of all, I would like to thank our four beautiful children, Christopher, Jennifer, Heidi and Holley, for the time and energy stolen from them throughout the years, without complaint, that I might serve others.

Contents:

Preface

*T*he *No-Nonsense Church* is written with all Christian churches in mind. The majority of churches wrestle, day in and day out, with overcoming the limitations of their size and resources. In the pages of *The No-Nonsense Church* all churches will discover affirmation that true success is found in the retention of the essential characteristics of the Body of Christ, not in the political maneuverings of the few or the support of the masses. Mega churches will find in these pages a sober call to resist the pressures of success that tempt God's people to compromise or lay aside the revealed will of God. Liberal minded churches will hopefully call into question any opposition to the clarity expressed in God's Word. Conservative minded churches will hopefully call into question any blind following after lifeless traditions and rituals.

The No-Nonsense Church is a call for every Christian ministry to reject the nonsense of the world in the light of the pure wisdom from above. Every true individual Christian, who is, by the default of God's grace, a member of Christ's Body, will hopefully and prayerfully find reason to recommit him/herself to an abiding dependent faith in Christ, faithfully serving others as his ambassador on earth. I have included questions at the end of each chapter in order to facilitate digging deeper into the truth revealed in God's Word. I hope that small groups may find it beneficial in their prayerful discussions of the truths presented in *The No-Nonsense Church.*

My attempt to distinguish between the universal visible Body of Christ, made up of all believers, and individual congregations is noted by the use of a capital C for the former. I have intentionally chosen to include extensive Biblical references as endnotes to encourage the reader to become familiar with what God has said about the subject, without bogging down the text itself. I encourage all readers to look up the passages in their own Bibles and to study them in their original context. Only what God has said gives credence to the message of this book.

Introduction: Wake-Up Call!

"Rid yourselves of all the offenses you have committed,
and get a new heart and a new spirit.
Why will you die, O house of Israel?" Ezekiel 18:31

Walking out of church, worship having just ended, a member is overheard saying, "Oh great, it's G__ d____ hot again!" How could such abominable words flow freely off of the lips of someone who just lifted up praise and worship to God? Hypocritical behavior is rampant in the churches of Jesus Christ. And we may observe it everywhere.

God's people have always wrestled with sin, but the growing apathy and intensifying evil present in the visible Body of Christ is phenomenal. Churches, along with their pastors, are promoting the most atrocious behaviors under the Christian banner. Right and left, congregations are misconstruing the grace of God. On the left, liberal churches seem bent on ridding sin of its stigma, as though grace grants immoral liberty.

On the right, conservative churches often fall into the traps of legalism. Legalism falsely conveys obedience as a way to receive the grace and blessings of Christ. Other conservatives fail to confront sin in fear of the legalistic stigma and, thereby, misrepresent the call of God upon his people to reject sin and obey his law. Faithfulness continues to be God's call upon all believers, even though obedience is entirely God's work of grace. Still others may become so fixated on the doctrinal correctness of grace that they inadvertently convey a discouragement of personal testimonies, which provides evidence of God's work of grace. These churches seem to forget that the power and grace of God in Christ actually changes the heart so as to enable God's people to believe, make decisions, and behave in defiance of the natural self.

Both the law of God and the Gospel of Jesus Christ are misrepresented and confused. The result is churches out of control. Why else may it be readily observed, in both liberal and conservative churches, a membership plagued with divorce, ungodly lifestyles, and unbridled tongues? Why else do congregations, across the spectrum of theology, engage in devouring those sent to serve them? While clergy and their families are strangled emotionally, denominational executives and their representatives appear to stand aloof in fear of congregational division. Out of fear of rocking the boat, the most appalling behaviors are ignored.

In the same illogical vein as those who view rape victims as responsible for their plight, abused clergy are viewed as having brought on the injustices they encounter. The church and her workers need to remember that no one is to return evil for evil.[1] Both, congregations and clergy, are called to have the same mind and attitude as Jesus Christ.[2]

One after another, congregations are becoming pathetic examples of how not to treat each other. God's people toss aside the fruit of the Spirit and succumb to bitterness, anger, and hatred. Polluted by the stinking thinking of the world, many in the church have adopted sin as something to embrace.

Intensifying the destructive forces at work in the church are clergy who themselves abuse those they are sent to serve. Abominable violations of clergy trust are exemplified in the widespread scandals of the Roman Catholic Church. We may again observe situations where denominational officials attempt to ignore or cover up such dark behaviors instead of bringing them to light. Recurrently, accountability is no longer a call to truth and right behavior, but instead a call to tolerate what is wrong in the name of a false sense of peace.

God forewarned that many Christians would claim allegiance to Christ while disregarding His teachings. Sin will always endanger the fellowship of believers, as long as sin remains. Satan will continually seek entrance into the church rising up his henchman in opposition to the Spirit of Christ. Only churches gracing the essential characteristics of the Body of Christ are equipped to effectively resist and overcome the evil that brings destruction. Paul's admonition to individuals ought to be applied to every congregation as well; "Examine yourselves to see whether you are in the faith; test yourselves."[3]

An insidious poison is being injected into mainstream Christianity. A rising insurgence is seeking to decapitate the head of the Body, Jesus Christ. Without the head, the body dies. The ecumenical movement has been swept off its feet by this poison. What possible value is derived from peaceful relationships between dead bodies? This poison originates from the same evil one that instigates Islamic insurgents to decapitate their enemies in the name of Allah. We live in a world of nonsense. I pray that God opens the eyes of churches to see the handwriting on the wall.

Congregations are not necessarily to blame for individual member's hypocrisies. All churches ought to be engaged in no-nonsense ministry where sin is confronted and the Gospel of Jesus Christ is conveyed in all of its beauty and relevance. Whenever ministry loses the strength of the law of God and the power of the Gospel of Jesus Christ nonsense follows. Testimonials concerning the widespread epidemic of churches that are majoring in the trivial and neglecting the purpose for which Christ organized His people are all too common.

The 16th century Protestant Reformation called upon the church to return to the central truths, expressed in the Holy Scriptures of God. Christianity is founded upon the rock of Jesus Christ. Fed by the word of truth, handed down from the prophets and apostles, and empowered by the Holy Spirit of God, churches define their existence. Whenever God's people no longer hunger to hear the truth of Christ, they become entangled in ministry of sheer nonsense.

How many churches have become torn apart over issues that were irrelevant to the message and mission of the church? Issues that involve arguing for one's pet peeves, holding to a form of religion while denying its power, and confusing the truth by insisting on adherence to man made traditions. Denominations may be divided over theological understandings of God and his Word, but the members of congregations are more likely divided over selfish opinionated decisions. Too many Christians walk away from the fellowship of the church because they didn't get their way.

Throughout history, organizations develop and fall into various holes and ruts. Time and again, the church spends her energy maintaining what is severely broken. Adhering to long-standing routines and rituals, churches may become blinded to the real needs and opportunities to share the Gospel of Christ. Tempted by society's ills and tolerant thinking, churches succumb to the pressures of this world by elevating those principles that appear to be financially beneficial and politically correct.

Churches that become engaged in behavior clearly condemned by the message of God produces an even greater concern. Behaviors, such as gossiping and slandering of one another, cast aside love and bond the members of a church in hate. Churches abound whose members engage in manipulating and controlling behavior of one another out of a selfish need for power and recognition. Members provide leadership in the church in order to give voice to their baggage of anger and bitterness. Others seek to control, since in the world they seem to have lost all control.

Inappropriately condemning and judging brothers and sisters in Christ has become standard procedure for many Christians. Refusal to join in the study of God's Word, or to give generously, is common in all churches. Churches sabotage the work of God's Spirit and bring destruction upon the Body, gathered in the Name of Christ, by casting aside God's Word.

The worldly attitude and mindset, that has long replaced the Lordship of Christ in many ministries, is not novel. The early Christian churches wrestled with much of the same struggles, as the present day church. James admonishes his readers, "You want something but don't get it. You kill and covet, but you cannot have what you want. You quarrel and fight. You do not have, because you do not ask God. When you ask, you do not receive; because you ask with wrong motives, that you may spend what you get on your pleasures. You adulterous people, don't you know that friendship with the world is hatred toward God?"[4]

The Christian Church will continue to engage a mix of those who mouth the teachings of Christ with those who genuinely confess the faith. In the end, Christ Himself will separate the weeds from the wheat.[5] Nevertheless, the inevitable presence of hypocrites does not mean churches are to ignore the rampant ungodliness that seeks to hide under the disguise of the ministry. God's people are to confront, admonish and separate from blatant sin. Too many churches are being duped by the flesh, deceived by Satan, and reprogrammed by the world.

God's Word enables us to identify good from evil, so that we are equipped to properly reject sin. God's Spirit works discernment, through the Word, so that God's people may turn to him in true repentance and live by faith in the truth of Christ. Any ministry that has laid aside the law and Gospel messages of God's Word to strive after a man made love and peace, unity or harmony, has taken a detour off the path of life in Christ and is drowning in worldly nonsense. To those churches the message is clear; "Repent and return unto the Lord!"

For far too long the Christian Church has been drifting towards nonsense. Further and further away from her roots in the teachings of the Apostles, the church today often looks more like the church of the apostasy. This book paints the image of no-nonsense ministries by bringing to light the basic characteristics that are absolutely essential for the faithful of God to adorn.

Unquestionably, because of the fallen nature of man living in a fallen world, the Church is a hospital for sinners, not a haven for saints. This reality colors the Church's expectation of perfection, this side of heaven. One anticipates that the ministry will engage those who have not yet reached the height of maturity. The people of God are bonded together in their need to receive the truth, as Christ simultaneously commissions them to convey his truth to the world around them.

There is no perfect fellowship of believers, just as there is no perfect man, save Jesus Christ alone. My desire in writing this book is to offer Biblical clarity and stimulation towards the recognition and rejection of the world's nonsense in the affairs of a congregation. Too much nonsense has infected the ministry of our Lord Jesus. Many churches are, at best, surviving, and at worst, dying. This is a terrible testimony to the power and grace, love and mercy of our Savior.

I pray this message serves to inspire the Body of Christ in fulfilling her mission. All no-nonsense *Christian* ministries are first and foremost driven by faith in Jesus Christ. The clear mission of the Church is to share the Gospel of Christ with the world in which she lives.

In the simplest form, the strategy for sharing the love of Christ, individually or collectively, consists of being "in the Word, on one's knees, and looking beyond the self to others." As long as the church is Christ centered, Word grounded, Spirit empowered, faith driven, love motivated, relationship oriented, and mission focused, she will exemplify the generosity of God's love through spiritual leadership and will battle successfully in the war against evil that she finds herself. This book is written with the hope of promoting such no-nonsense ministry in the Christian Church.

Endnotes

[1] 1 Peter 3:8
[2] Philippians 2:1-5
[3] 2 Corinthians 13:5
[4] James 4:1-4
[5] Matthew 13:24-30

Chapter 1 – Christ Centered
(or "What Were We Thinking?")

*"Let us fix our eyes on Jesus,
the author and perfecter of our faith" Hebrews 12:2a*

Every Easter Christians gather together in the church of Jesus Christ proclaiming the truth of his resurrection. We announce to the world, "Christ is alive!" And because he is alive – we too are alive. But are we? Are we truly alive in his name? Are our churches alive?

Christians are Easter people! The Church is a fellowship of people resurrected out of the dead world. Christians live in defiance of this present evil age because they have been rescued from darkness and transported into the light of God's presence, but death continues to haunt all of us.[1] Is there anyone who imagines that he or she is immune from the shadow of death?

Consider that death lurks around every corner. Always hangs over our heads. Always threatens our existence and our enjoyments. Sin and death threaten to rob us of our peace and steal from us the joy of our blessings. Death is a real enemy that seeks to destroy our lives in Christ. Does *anyone* dispute death's reality?

And just what does the shadow of death entail? A woman wakes up one morning and feels a lump. And in that moment life is threatened. Overnight, people become victims of disease, accidents, and tragedies. Unexpected, unprepared, shocked, and traumatized, death seems to have the final say.

Young or old, Christian or unbeliever, death threatens our lives. Parents worry and live in fear because they know that their children are not immune from death's grip. Consider the child, full of zest and energy, who, in the midst of laughing and playing, runs out into the street and no longer walks the earth. The teenager, maturing, growing, inspiring, gets behind the wheel of a car and drives into eternity. Parents are provided with no warning. Those loved and cherished are here one day and gone the next.

And consider how we grow old. Everything may be going well in life until one schedules a routine physical and ends up under the surgeon's knife. In an instant, life changes as death squeezes any opportunities for living. Little by little, life is drained from our bodies. The aging process will catch up to all of us, if death does not lock us into its grip before we grow old. Who can escape the jaws of death?

This curse of sin does not just affect our bodies, but our souls as well. Depression has become such a prevalent experience of humanity. Whether caused by physical and chemical deficiencies, emotional trauma, situational tragedies, or genetics, depression is a direct result of one's body and mind being held in the bondage of death. Depression surely isn't how God created us to think or feel.

Nor did God create us to be anxious and full of worry or to be driven by fears and doubts or to experience grief and pain and disappointments. Nor can we get rid of this death grip enslaving our minds and emotions simply through faith and forgiveness, any more than we can rid our bodies of cancer and other dreaded diseases by simply increasing our faith and repenting of our sins. We are born into a dying world enslaved by the power of sin and death.[2] Left to ourselves we would be lost forever.[3]

Our gracious God may choose to provide temporary healing in this world, when and where he pleases, but healing in one area does not mean death has lost it's touch upon our lives. We still grow old, we still get sick, and we still die, even as Lazarus was raised from the grave only to die again. No-nonsense ministries have a single-minded focus, to bring a resurrected Christ to a world ensnared by sin and death.

The message that proclaims victory over death is not some trivial message. The Gospel of Jesus Christ is THE message of life. The resurrection provides THE hope of existence. Jesus Christ is

THE life source of the ministry and THE foundation upon which the church builds all aspects of her ministry. That is why Easter is THE high point of Christian worship. The resurrection of Christ is the backdrop of the Great Commission of our Lord.[4]

The living presence of Christ gives credence to the purpose of the church's existence.[5] "And if Christ has not been raised, our preaching is useless and so is your faith."[6] God's people gather to worship and serve him who alone is the Lord of lords and King of kings.[7]

Christ is alive! He is the Lion of the tribe of Judah, the Root of David, the lamb having been slain.[8] This is the Easter victory and in this reality the church finds her truest identity. Take away the death and resurrection of Christ and the church loses her mission and meaning. When Christ, hanging on the cross, cried out – "It is finished," sin and the father of sin, the devil, were defeated. The last enemy to be defeated was death.[9] And when this final enemy bit the dust at the resurrection of Jesus Christ then the eternal happiness of all who believe was forever set in stone.[10]

Maybe there exists a level of civic appropriateness for governments and politicians to reference God by the limited generic vision of his identity as Creator. Surely God has created all. In the civic arena, God may be referenced according to his law or his love that holds applicable for the whole of humanity. But, the Christian Church has the specific responsibility to clarify the person of God, as he is known through the Messiah, Jesus Christ. Whenever any Christian pastor speaks, he does so as a representative of Christ himself.

Any Christian ministry that becomes distracted away from the Christological nature of her message spins her wheels in nonsense. There is no other gospel.[11] Ultimately, death will have a say in everything the church experiences in this veil of tears. "But take heart," Jesus reminds us, "I have overcome this world."[12]

A tragic sadness descends upon Christianity as terrorism, the newest face of the enemy, strikes a level of fear never before experienced upon the face of the earth. No longer identified with nationality, this enemy threatens all nations. In the frenzy of fear, created by insecurity and unrest, the fever for peace rises. Fever typically indicates that the body is fighting an infectious intruder. When the intrusion is greater than the body can fight, the prolonged fever rises to dangerous levels whereby the fever itself endangers the body.

The legitimate fever for peace seeks to fight the insidious hatred between nations and races. The Christian's desire for peace is driven by faith in Christ. When fear and not faith drives the frenzy for peace, then the fever takes on a dimension that loses the foundation upon which appropriate peace is built. This gives way to an even greater threat.

The deceiver will lure the world into a false sense of peace aimed at quieting the very spirit of terrorism that his spirit stimulated. Satan has an even higher aim than the destructive acts of terrorism. In order to quiet the raging fears that grip our broken world, there will be an increased demand for tolerance. I don't believe it's merely coincidental that terrorism has risen within a religious context.

Hate crimes will continue to muddy the waters of necessary moral convictions. Intolerance will increasingly become identified as the real enemy. The intolerance of terrorism serves to promote the tolerance ideology aimed specifically *against* religion as a whole.

As the fever for peace rises to unprecedented proportions, the persecuted will become those with religious integrity. Christ did predict that war and rumors of wars were only the beginning of birth pains.[13] According to God, the end will come when the world is proclaiming safety and peace.[14]

"Fear not!" Christ repeatedly comforts his followers. John affirms, "Then he placed his right hand on me and said: 'Do not be afraid. I am the First and the Last. I am the Living One; I was dead, and behold I am alive forever and ever! And I hold the keys of death and Hades.'" [15]

God Almighty proclaims that his Son is "the image of the invisible God, the firstborn over all creation. For by him all things were created: things in heaven and on earth, visible and invisible, whether thrones or powers or rulers or authorities; all things were created by him and for him. He is before all things, and in him all things hold together. And he is the head of the body, the church; he is the beginning and the firstborn from among the dead, so that in everything he might have the supremacy. For God was pleased to have all his fullness dwell in him, and through him to reconcile to himself all things, whether things on earth or things in heaven, by making peace through his blood, shed on the cross."[16]

God is anything but indifferent concerning the world's view of his Son. Do we think the Father does not care in whom the world finds salvation? Can we possibly conclude that Jesus is the way for only the Gentile Church in this dispensation! Jesus is the only way to salvation. All of history is *His Story*! All of creation was made by him and for him. Regardless of the era or time period, the life of God's people is discovered in the Messiah. Jesus is the most indescribable gift of God's love.[17]

John received an incredible revelation of Christ. "When I saw him, I fell at his feet as though dead."[18] John's vision of the glorious risen Christ literally knocked the breath out of him. He could no longer stand on his own two feet. The beauty and power and majesty of the world's Savior overwhelmed his entire body/soul/spirit presence and down he went. This very same Christ, alive and glorified, presents himself to those who believe in his name. Collectively, we are called the Christian Church. Paul refers to the fellowship of believers as the Body of Christ.

For us to operate as the Body of Christ, Jesus must remain center-stage. When one attends an outdoor music festival there are usually multiple stages set up. There is always an identifiable main stage. On the main stage the most sought after artists are performing. In the Christian Church, Jesus Christ is center-stage on the main stage. All worship, all proclamations, all teachings point his way and no other way is allowed to distract or confuse away from the Lord of the Church.

If any church desires to travel life's journey with Christ, then the Lord of lords must be in the driver's seat. To push him to the back seat may prove more dangerous than kicking him out of the car entirely because it produces a false sense of security. If we are to return to paradise, we will not get there from here unless the King himself delivers us.

The most dangerous teaching today is the politically correct propaganda that Jesus Christ is not the only way to salvation. Any church promoting this heresy is doomed from the get go. If she is not destroyed prior to, then she will certainly reap destruction at the 2nd coming of the Son of Man. The Revelation of John may be crouched in mystery, but one thing remains clear throughout this profound vision: In the end, those who oppose the Son of God at his appearing will be cast into the lake of fire.

The summer between high school and college I lived with my brother in an apartment. I was only 18 years of age. One evening, heading for bed, I noticed the parking lot lamp outside my window had been broken and my room was unusually dark. In the middle of the night I awoke to a firm hand shaking my shoulder. Awaking from sleep, I assumed my brother wanted something. Turning around to see what he wanted I immediately beheld the most satisfying vision ever. There at the foot of the bed stood the Lord in radiant light. My entire room was lit. Goose bumps crept up my body, beginning with my feet to my head. The smile that graced my face was so intense that I thought the corners of my lips were touching my ears. A joy and peace filled my being.

How do I know if it was truly the Lord? I don't. I only know that no words were spoken and I'll never forget the experience. Because I do not possess faith due to my experience nor received any directives that sought to guide me, there is really no need to question my memory. This I know, with or without the experience: Jesus is alive and is Lord over all!

The church is ALL about Jesus! If not, then who? No, it's *all* about Jesus! Any Christian congregation who fails to draw her identity from Christ has lost her place among the lamp stands.[19] Christ is not just the reason for the season of Christmas; Christ is the reason for the existence of the Christian Church. She is his body; the collective confession originally confessed by Peter, "You are the Christ, the Son of the Living God."[20]

Christ is the authoritative head. His presence gives life to the Body.[21] His authority empowers the presence of the Body.[22] Apart from Christ there is no living corpus Christi. A Christ-less church is a dead organism waiting for destruction. Christ is the foundation.[23] He is the focus of the Church's preaching.[24] Christ is the object of the Spirit's gifts distributed among God's people.[25]

Sitting in the pew of a small English speaking Christian church, the counterpart of the larger main church in Bratislava, Slovakia, on what was termed World Religion Sunday, I was shocked at what was being preached. I was astounded to hear the ramblings of a sermon that accused Christianity today of bigotry because it is taught that the Christian religion is the only way to God. In a very clear and articulate delivery, this Christian pastor denied Jesus Christ as the only Savior of the world and the only way to the Father. Such confident conclusions lie only in the desperations of a lost church. Universalistic teachings are logical deductions void of the Spirit of the living Christ.

There is no other Savior given to the world whereby we can be saved. Jesus said, "Whoever believes in the Son has eternal life, but whoever rejects the Son will not see life, for God's wrath remains on him."[26] Through John, God enlightens his people to the nature of the anti-Christ. He says, "This is how you can recognize the Spirit of God: Every spirit that acknowledges that Jesus Christ has come in the flesh is from God, but every spirit that does not acknowledge Jesus is not from God. This is the spirit of the antichrist, which you have heard is coming and even now is already in the world." [27] Jesus reflected to his disciples, "He who is not with me is against me, and he who does not gather with me scatters."[28] There is no other Name.[29]

There is a popular belief held by many, in defiance of Scriptural truth, concerning the name of God. In various forms this belief states, "All religions simply call God by different names." Actually this teaching is hardly new. Mohammed, the founder of Islam, taught, already in the 7th century, that the Jewish and Christian religions believed in the same one God as Islam. The revered "holy" book of Islam, the Koran, even references Jesus almost a hundred times.[30] However, in doing so, Islam firmly denies that Jesus was himself God or that Jesus was the Savior of the world.

Anyone familiar with Biblical writings knows how much emphasis God, throughout both the Old and New Testaments, placed upon the names used to reveal his identity and work. So precious was the name, Yahweh, conveyed to Moses, that the Israelites would not even say it out loud. After forbidding his people to recognize any other gods or make images of any other gods, God forbade his people to misuse his Name.[31] The world may not place much stock in the specific references to God's names, but God's people know him by the names that he uses to describe who and what he has done.

Christianity bows to the seductive lies of Satan whenever other gods are incorporated into God's identity. Christianity is also perverted when God's self-revelation is altered so as to proclaim multiple ways to salvation. A great blindness is falling upon much of Christianity. God's people are being deceived whenever it is taught that the Father can be separated from the Son in true worship and allegiance. Directing his words to those of the Jewish religion, Christ emphatically stated, "You do not know me or my Father."[32] Jesus proclaimed, "He who hates me hates my Father as well."[33]

We worship the Father only through the Son. Those who claim allegiance to the God of the Old Testament while denying the God of the New Testament worship in ignorance. The God of Abraham sent his Son and those who reject the Son have rejected the Father.[34] John the Baptist admonished the Jewish leaders saying, "And do not think you can say to yourselves, 'We have Abraham as our father.' I tell you that out of these stones God can raise up children for Abraham."[35] According to Jesus, those who deny Christ as the Messiah have denied the truth of the Old Testament Scriptures.[36]

In the same vein, the Apostle John makes it plain, in no uncertain terms, that denial of the Son is denial of the Father who sent the Son. He says, "Who is the liar? It is the man who denies that Jesus is the Christ. Such a man is the antichrist – he denies the Father and the Son. No one who denies the Son has the Father; whoever acknowledges the Son has the Father also."[37] In clear exhortation, John declares, "Everyone who believes that Jesus is the Christ is born of God, and everyone who loves the Father loves his child as well."[38]

Even the 20th century Swiss theologian, Karl Barth, proclaimed the unique revelation of God in Jesus Christ. During his Princeton's Lectures, a student asked him whether God had revealed himself in other religions, as well as Christianity. Barth replied emphatically that God had not revealed himself in any religion. He had revealed himself only in his Son, Jesus Christ.

According to the first chapter in Romans, we recognize that the natural knowledge of God may lead certain non-Christians to place faith in one God. However, such faith is far from saving faith. Only in God's self-revelation are we able to discern God's identity and plan of salvation through Jesus Christ. Otherwise, God's love remains unknown.

In the identity of the one true God, the Father, Son or Holy Spirit cannot be excluded. Though the persons of the Trinity are separate and distinct from each other, there is no God apart from all three.[39] Jesus proclaimed that if one had seen him, then he had seen the Father.[40] The Father is known through the Son.[41] Jesus declared that the Father and the Son are one.[42] Our Lord cried out, "When a man believes in me, he does not believe in me only, but in the one who sent me."[43]

In the end, those victorious over Satan stand with the Lamb of God on Mount Zion, sealed by the Spirit, and on their foreheads are written the names of BOTH the Father AND the Son.[44] How arrogant of those who claim allegiance to Christ to rewrite the truth claims of the One who died for the world.[45] Do Christians really believe that the Father, who was separated from his only Son in death so that the world might have life, is indifferent to whether his people acknowledge his Son as the Redeemer of mankind?

Paul directs his words to the Christians of Galatia: "Grace and peace to you from God our Father and the Lord Jesus Christ who gave his life for our sins to rescue us from the present evil age, according to the will of our God and Father, to whom be glory forever and ever. Amen."[46] Then this Jewish Christian apostle of our Lord proceeds to declare in one of the clearest and yet sobering warnings of the New Testament, "I am astonished that you are so quickly deserting the one who called you by the grace of Christ and are turning to a different gospel – which is really no gospel at all. Evidently some people are throwing you into confusion and are trying to pervert the gospel of Christ. But even if we or an angel from heaven should preach a gospel other than the one we preached to you, let him be eternally condemned! As we have already said, so now I say again: If anybody is preaching to you a gospel other than what you accepted, let him be eternally condemned!"[47]

The exclusive claims of Christianity will always fly in the face of the world's political correctness. When Jesus proclaimed; "I am the way, the truth and the life, no one comes to the Father except through me," he was laying the foundation for the exclusiveness of his message of salvation.[48] Although the way to salvation excludes those who refuse to place their hope in Christ, the invitation of salvation is anything but exclusive. "Go and make disciples of all nations," is all inclusive.[49] Christ died for all that *all* might live. And though many refuse to "get it right," or to accept the exclusive claims of Christ, even among his claimed followers, the Gospel continues to speak the revelation of God.

The first century Jews got it right with respect to this. They understood well that one either places his faith in Jesus as the Messiah or one stones Him to death.[50] In response to Jesus acclamation that he was one with the Father, the Bible says, "Again the Jews picked up stones to stone him."[51] The idea that Jesus is one of many ways to salvation or one of many names leading to the Father is completely overturned by Scripture's clear testimony, "There is no other name given to men by which we must be saved."[52]

When man chose to rebel against the Creator by his arrogant disobedience, all of creation fell under the curse of God. The Almighty vowed to undo the curse by virtue of his own commitment to humanity. God so loved that he gave. Through his own Son's defeat over sin, death, and the devil, God won victory for all of mankind. That was God's plan from the beginning.[53]

God reveals his original promise of a deliverer in Genesis 3:15. Speaking to the tempter God says, "And I will put enmity between you and the woman, and between your offspring and hers; he will crush your head and you will strike his heel." Now if the deliverer was to come through a male offspring of the woman and Christ is identified as the fulfillment of that original Gospel promise, then the claim of deliverance by any other seed or any other way is false.

Holding to the belief that God's Spirit will in the end open the eyes and hearts of thousands of Jewish people in a mass conversion is an entirely different matter than believing that a Jew stands approved by God apart from faith in Christ. God rejected Old Testament Israelites who rejected his works of salvation. Jesus, denouncing the Jewish cities "in which most of his miracles had been performed, because they did not repent," said that it would be more bearable for Tyre, Sidon, and Sodom on the Day of Judgment then upon them.[54]

The value in recognizing that the natural knowledge of God may lead other religions to acknowledge the one God lies in the church's mission. Christians, like Paul, may use such recognition to connect with non-Christians in the hope of making known the will of God in Christ toward them. While walking among the idols of Athens, Paul came across an altar to an unknown God. Using this as a Gospel handle, Paul said, "Now what you worship as something unknown I am going to proclaim to you."[55] In order to reach Islam with the Gospel message is the reason why some Christians suggest that Allah shouldn't be referred to as a false god.[56]

Conceding the natural knowledge of the true God in no way recognizes other religions as pleasing to God. Those who reject Christ are not the children of God. Jesus said, "If God were your Father, you would love me, for I came from God and now am here."[57] Jesus further stated to the Jews who rejected Him, "The reason you do not hear is that you do not belong to God."[58]

Christians also display ludicrous thinking by suggesting that non-Christians are children of the Heavenly Father because they are "good people," though they reject the Son of God. Such teachings convey a blatant concept of work righteousness contrary to the central Christian teaching that we are saved through faith in Jesus Christ by the grace of God. Salvation is not a gift given to "good people" but to "poor sinners" by a graciously good God because of the death of his Son.[59]

What a sham that so many Christian churches have lost their allegiance to the only Savior of the world. The only God that the true Christian trusts is the God who "gave his one and only Son, that whoever believes in him shall not perish but have eternal life."[60] Just what part of this Gospel in a nutshell no longer applies? God sent his One and ONLY begotten Son to become one of us, to die as a sin-payment for the world, so that *all* might be saved.[61]

Jesus has revealed himself as the way to salvation. I stand in amazement of how far ministries bearing the name of Christ are drifting from his clear testimony. What is offensive to God's own people about their Lord's worldwide revelation? The fact that many reject the truth doesn't make the truth true for only a select few. Rejection of the truth doesn't make the truth any less true, only inapplicable for those who choose to refuse the great salvation, purchased by the blood of the sacrificial Lamb. The generous God of love does not demand our love in return, only enables it by interjecting his power, love and grace into a world of darkness.

When the church's ministry becomes different than the ministry of our Savior, something has gone grossly astray. "Go and make disciples of ALL nations!" is the Lord's directive to his followers to reach out to *all* with *his* truth and make disciples devoted to Christ. Our mission is to make Christ-lovers of all nations, not merely lovers of people or of animals and trees. We are not offered salvation by way of loving the creation. Our mission is not to make peace with other religions, but to bring the peace of Christ to a fallen world. We are saved through faith in a loving God who gave himself to a dying world by way of his Son, our Savior, Jesus Christ, who embodies the essence of true life.

Disciples are committed to Christ and therefore to the truth of Christ. "The whole truth and nothing but the truth." Christ sent the members of his church out into the world to bring the truth of God, "teaching them to obey everything I have commanded you."[62] How can those who have been enlisted in the service of the King pick and choose which of the King's teachings are valuable and which are insignificant?

Shall we change our commission by adding or subtracting to the truth once delivered through the prophets and apostles in order to express a more tolerant message to the 21st century? If the goal of ministry is to build big churches, raise a lot of money, and avoid giving offense, then perverting the message, as a means to an end, might seem justified. But, the goal of ministry is to build relationships upon the rock of Christ, which by nature is offensive to a worldly view of life.[63] In no-nonsense ministries all other goals are subservient to the proclamation of Christ.[64] Any goal not serving this primary aim of ministry ought to be declined as superficial and contrary to the proper stewardship of the Body.

The tolerant philosophy of so many Christian churches that rewrites the truth claims of God simply does not cut it. A church may be very successful in the eyes of society at doing her own thing, but that is a far cry from her calling. The church is called to do "Christ's thing," nothing more and nothing less. How can the Body of Christ live in denial of her head?[65] And not just the head of the Body but "head over everything for the church, which is his body, the fullness of him who fills everything in every way."[66]

No-nonsense ministry returns time and time again, endlessly, to insure that Jesus Christ lives in the very heart of life. Christ is seated at the right hand of the Father "far above all rule and authority, power and dominion, and every title that can be given, not only in the present age but also in the one to come."[67] Point me to one other prophet or religious leader who is declared to be above all powers and authorities. The life of Christ is the heart beat of the church. If the momentum of any congregation beats to a different drummer other than Jesus, it beats down the wrong path.

Forget whether this is palatable to the world. Of course it isn't. God has declared the Gospel of Jesus Christ to be a stumbling block.[68] In the same absurd vein as requiring the Boy Scouts to include girls, or shelters for battered women to include men, the world presses their nonsense upon the Christian Church to recognize all religions as legitimate paths to everlasting life. But, her identity and her mission define the Christian Church. Christians are followers of the world's Savior, Jesus Christ, with the specified mission to share this truth with the rest of humanity.

Where did all of the teachings of nonsense creep into the churches of our Lord? Satan has had a hey day with the infiltration of his garbled doctrines of tolerance. How can Jesus be the great teacher and simultaneously a misdirected prophet at best, or a psychotic liar, at worst? If Jesus is not THE Way, then he was an egomaniac. How can those who claim allegiance to Christ disclaim his teachings? What kind of nonsense is that?

This by no means gives way to the hatred expressed by confused, embittered, angry religious fanatics. The spirit that lives in Islamic terrorists who despise infidels, as well as the spirit that lives in Christian terrorists who blow up abortion clinics, is not from God. We are to fight with the sword of the Spirit, which is the Word of God.[69] And in doing so, we are to have as our aim the salvation of all.

With tact and gentleness, love and commitment, we are to bring the power of the Gospel of Jesus Christ to ALL because God so loved ALL that he gave to ALL his only begotten Son. We are to love those who persecute us, spit on us, or say all kinds of things against us because of Jesus.[70] We are to love them by proclaiming Christ in word and deed. That is our mission as representatives of Jesus Christ. That is not the mission of the government. That is the mission of the Church.

Jesus taught that there is no other way to the Father. Jesus points to himself and proclaims, "I am the way and the truth and the life. No one comes to the Father except through me."[71] In truth, this is the teaching that distinguishes him from the entire spectrum of world religious leaders. The latter merely pointed towards a way to the divine. The truth claims of Jesus are insane unless he is the divine Son of God incarnate? Jesus affirmed that one is either for him or against him.[72] God confirmed that those who do not receive Christ in faith perish.[73] If what Christ taught was wrong, then he was wrong. If churches believe that what Jesus taught was mistaken then why do they place so much emphasis, time, and money in allegiance to him? Is that not ludicrous?

And if sin is no longer viewed as sin, if condemning behavior of one's personal choices is no longer appropriate, what is the cross of Christ about? If sin is tolerated there is no need for forgiveness. If God could tolerate sin why send his Son to die a gruesome death upon a cross? When did the forgiveness of sin become equated with tolerance over sin? These two concepts are as far apart as the east is from the west. Why lift up a Savior who died for no apparent reason to free us from a hell that never really existed? So many Christians have totally lost any sense of sanity. Holding to Christ, countless Christians have no clue who he is, what he did, or why.

Asking the question, "What would Jesus do?" will not suffice. "What has Jesus done, what is he doing, and what does his great love compel us to do?" is more sufficient. Shall the light of Christ empower us for a new day or shall we continue to fumble our way in the darkness of yesterday? Maybe there are ministries that never thought in terms like this before. Great! A new day is dawning!

The Church's one foundation
Is Jesus Christ her Lord,
She is his new creation
By water and the Word.
From heav'n he came and sought her
To be his holy bride;
With his own blood he bought her
And for her life he died.
The Church shall never perish!
Her dear Lord to defend,
To guide, sustain, and cherish,
Is with her to the end:
Tho' there be those that hate her,
False sons within her pale,
Against both foe and traitor
She ever shall prevail.[74]

The fellowship of the no-nonsense Church is "with the Father and with his Son, Jesus Christ," in the power of the Holy Spirit.[75] The Church of Jesus Christ is absolutely firm in her allegiance to the Lamb of God! She does not sway in the Christological nature of her identity, her worship of the Trinity, her teachings of Scripture, or her confession of faith. She is the Bride of Christ and her loyalty to her Eternal Heavenly Groom, as the Author and Finisher of her faith, is without doubt, unmistakable and unshakable. The Body of Christ celebrates Jesus in all of her programs, activities, and relationships. Anything short of this is nonsense.

Digging Deeper into God's Word

1. Read Philippians 2:5-11. Since Christ has been exalted above every name, every knee will bow in homage to Jesus Christ, and every tongue confess Jesus to be Lord, what are the implications in this passage for any religious leader who refuses to acknowledge the supremacy of Christ? If the knees of Mohammed and Buddha, along with all others, will bow in confession of Christ,

how then should we treat the teachings of Christ with respect to the religious teachings of others?

2. Read Hebrews chapter 1. If everything is subject to Jesus, then what conclusion might be drawn concerning religions that deny Christ as the only way to the Father? Reread Hebrews 1:8. Does the author of Hebrews leave his readers with the impression that the Jewish rejection of Jesus Christ as the Messiah is an acceptable option for God's people?

3. Read 1 Corinthians 15:20-28. What does Paul's statements about the resurrected Christ reigning over all things after he has destroyed all dominion, authority and power imply about religions that oppose Christ as the Messiah and Savior of the world?

4. Read Galatians 1:6-12. Does Paul leave any room for a different Gospel message other than the Gospel of Jesus Christ? What does the passage say to those who want to compromise the truth of Jesus and allow for multiple ways of salvation?

5. Read 1 Timothy 2:5. What is a mediator? How is Christ a mediator between God and man? Why is Paul saying that Christ alone is the mediator provided? Paul's statement that there is one God and one mediator leads to what conclusion concerning religions that reject Jesus Christ as the only Savior of the world? Read 1 Peter 2:4-8. What is a cornerstone? Do you think there is more than one cornerstone?

6. Memorize Acts 4:12; "Salvation is found in no one else, for there is no other name under heaven given to men by which we must be saved."

Endnotes

[1] John 12:46

[2] Romans 8:6

[3] Ephesians 2:1-3

[4] Matthew 28:18-24

[5] See 1 Corinthians 15:14-19

[6] 1 Corinthians 15:14

[7] Revelation 19:16

[8] Revelation 5:5-6

[9] 1 Corinthians 15:26

[10] Philippians 3:20-21

[11] Galatians 1:6-7

[12] John 16:33

[13] Matthew 24:6-8

[14] 1 Thessalonians 5:3

[15] Revelation 1:17-18

[16] Colossians 1:15-20

[17] 2 Corinthians 9:15

[18] Revelation 1:17

[19] Revelation 2:10

[20] Matthew 16:16

[21] Ephesians 1:22-23

[22] Matthew 28:18

[23] 1 Corinthians 3:11

[24] 2 Corinthians 4:5

[25] Ephesians 4:11-13

[26] John 3:36

[27] 1 John 4:2-4

[28] Matthew 12:30

[29] Acts 4:12

[30] Ehlke, Roland Cap, Speaking the Truth in Love to Muslims, Northwestern Publishing House, Milwaukee, ©2004, p.63.

[31] Exodus 20:7

[32] John 8:19

[33] John 15:23

[34] Luke 10:16

[35] Matthew 3:9

[36] John 5:37-40

[37] 1 John 2:22-23

[38] 1 John 5:1

[39] Matthew 28:19

[40] John 14:9

[41] John 14:10

[42] John 10:30

[43] John 12:44

[44] Revelation 14:1

[45] John 4:44-49

[46] Galatians 1:3-5

[47] Galatians 1:6-9

[48] John 14:6

[49] Matthew 28:19

[50] Matthew 12:14

[51] John 10:31

[52] Acts 4:12

[53] Ephesians 1:4

[54] Matthew 11:20 (see verses 21-24)

[55] Acts 17:23b (see verses 16-31)

[56] Ehlke, Roland Cap, Speaking the Truth in Love to Muslims, Northwestern Publishing House, Milwaukee, ©2004, p.173

[57] John 8:42

[58] John 8:47

[59] Additional Christian teachings that disregard Christ as the only way to salvation is rooted in certain theological positions whereby Israel is viewed as being saved through a different covenant other than Christ.

[60] John 3:16

[61] Hebrews 9:26

[62] Matthew 28:20

[63] 1 Corinthians 1:20-23

[64] Philippians 1:18

[65] Colossians 1:8

[66] Ephesians 1:22

[67] Ephesians 1:21

[68] Romans 9:33 (cf. Isaiah 8:14; 28:16)

[69] Ephesians 6:17

[70] Matthew 5:43-48 (cf. Luke 6:27-36)

[71] John 14:6

[72] Matthew 12:30 (cf. Mark 9:40; Luke 9:50)

[73] Mark 16:16

[74] Samuel J. Stone, "The Church's One Foundation," 1866. public domain.

[75] 1 John 1:3

Chapter 2 – Word Grounded
(or "How Did We Get This Way?")

"Your word is a lamp to my feet and a light for my path."
Psalm 119:105

"This is my Son, whom I love. Listen to him."[1] When God the Father affirmed his love for the only begotten Son of God, Jesus Christ, he gave the disciples one succinct directive; "Listen to him." Can you imagine receiving a vision like the one given to John in revelation?[2] Now imagine that after having encountered the risen and glorified Christ you remain apathetic to His message. Imagine rising from having seen the King of kings and walking away to follow your own agenda of truth.

This same Christ who was transfigured before the eyes of Peter, James, and John, in the presence of Moses and Elijah, manifests himself to the Church through the proclamation and teaching of his Word. This is the very same Christ who by his appearance stopped a devout Jew named Saul on his path of exterminating Christians, and turned his life around so that he became Paul, the apostle to the Gentiles. Likewise, when the Holy Spirit brings the revelation of Christ home to the hearts of his people today, they listen. And they listen attentively as though the Master of the universe is speaking.

Having received the message of truth in Christ, no longer are God's people engulfed in the false. The Gospel of Christ has set them free. Years ago, at a conference for pastors and teachers, the conference speaker shared a story of "The Three Little Christians."[3] Here's my version:

Once there were three little church members, commissioned by their church to go out into the world and start new churches. So the three little church members set out on a journey to build other churches. As they went on their way they sang a popular song of their day: "Who's afraid of *The Way Life Is, The Way Life Is, The Way Life Is*, Who's afraid of *The Way Life Is*, Tra-la-la-la-la?

The first little church member took a right turn and ventured down a path into the past. He came upon a community that he determined to be a fine place to build a new church. Out of his bag he pulled all sorts of traditions, rules and rituals proven in the days gone by to have been effective in building churches. On these traditions, the first little church member built his church. The Bible was hailed as the source of all authority, but was actually secondary to the passion and energy spent on maintaining the church's traditions.

Everything went along fine until one day *The Way Life Is* came knocking on the door of the church. "Let me in!" demanded *The Way Life Is*. But the church was fearful of losing her traditions and refused to let *The Way Life Is* into her fellowship. However, *The Way Life Is* would not be locked out of the church. So *The Way Life Is* huffed and puffed until he forced entrance into the church and the church crumbled as her traditions were challenged and her foundations were declared obsolete.

The second little church member traveled farther down the path and took a left fork in the road. He came upon a very nice community whereby he could build a church. He too gave acknowledgment to the Bible as the source of the building plans. However, the second little church member was determined to build his church on the principle of love and good feelings. After all, if the church doesn't make one feel good, what good is it? Love, he concluded, was the bottom line of what the Bible teaches. So, the second little church member pulled out of his bag all sort of good feelings and he refused to tolerate any teaching or activity that threatened his definition of love.

The second little church member held to the teachings quoted by Paul, "'everything is permissible.'"[4] The intolerant spirit was labeled as the enemy of faith. Truth was declared to be a subjective reality. This meant that no one could teach a definitive truth to anyone else lest offense was given and love destroyed. The absolutes of truth were denied as archaic.

Great emphasis was placed upon "feeling good" so as to offend no one. Everything was going fine and the church was growing in great numbers until the day when *The Way Life Is* came knocking on the door of the church. "Little church, little church, let me come in," requested *The Way Life Is*. "Not by the hair of my chinny, chin, chin!" replied the 2nd little church member. "Then I'll huff and I'll puff and I'll blow your church down," threatened *The Way Life Is*."

Fearful that *The Way Life Is* would destroy the fellowship of love, the church refused to let *The Way Life Is* into her midst. *The Way Life Is* would not take no for an answer and huffed and puffed his way into the church's community, forcing her to define her love. *The Way Life Is* challenged the church's hypocritical toleration of certain teachings while refusing to tolerate others. And built on the foundation of undefined human love and good feelings the church fell, and great was her fall.

The third little church member found a nice place on the path he traveled to build a church. He set about, like the other two, to build a church upon the Bible. However, carrying no baggage, the third little church member marched to a different drummer. Whatever traditions from the past still served to promote the understanding of the Word, the third little church member sought to maintain. Whatever distracted from or confused the truth of God's Word, the third little church member sought to change. Love was defined by the truth of God's Word and the Bible was lifted up as a divine revelation from God. Great emphasis was placed on hearing what God had to say. And the church grew and matured in her faith and fellowship in Christ.

When *The Way Life Is* came knocking upon her door she did not fear *The Way Life Is*. She opened the door and welcomed *The Way Life Is* in. Here and there, *The Way Life Is* would yell and scream and make a fuss, but that is just *The Way Life Is*! The church built upon the Rock of Christ would quiet *The Way Life Is* with the Gospel of peace and promises in Christ.

Tragically, too many churches hang so tight to traditions, which have served the church well in years gone by, that they are dangerously close to fulfilling Scripture's admonishment about "having a form of godliness but denying its power."[5] Other churches are dangerously close to building upon the sinking sand without any foundational substance. They are fast becoming the church of the new age, the church of toleration. With ecumenical determination, many churches have called for tolerance by simply declaring undefined love to be the only thing that matters.

In similar fashion, the politically correct agenda of the world promotes the same ideology. Talking recently with a politician, in response to a sermon I preached that proclaimed Christ as the only way to salvation, this former senator declared that intolerance is the primary enemy of freedom. Generic declarations sound great on the surface, but they remain without substance.

Just what does it mean that tolerance is the friend of freedom. Tolerance for child molestation or abuse, tolerance for criminal activities, just what are we to tolerate? The politically correct judgment condemning the intolerant spirit cannot hold substance precisely because if it did it would cease to be tolerant. Consequently, this new teaching will continue to be generically espoused and applied primarily against the intolerance of religious integrity.

In contrast, Jesus declared that the one who is able to sustain the winds and rains and floods of any time period is the one who builds his/her life on the rock – the rock of his teachings. Hear what Christ had to say: "Therefore everyone who hears these words of mine and puts them into practice is like a wise man who built his house on the rock. The rain came down, the streams rose, and the winds blew and beat against that house; yet it did not fall, because it had its foundation on the rock. But everyone who hears these words of mine and does not put them into practice is like a foolish man who built his house on sand. The rain came down, the streams rose, and the winds blew and beat against that house, and it fell with a great crash."[6]

In spite of the clear warnings of Christ, studies have revealed how bogus it has become for the majority of Americans to still call themselves Christian. The name that once insured a commitment to a Biblical worldview, even if the exactness of such a view was highly debated, has become more attached to those who reject the teachings of Scripture, then those who hold them sacred.[7] The name Christian no longer insures a total commitment to Christ or to God's Word.

Standing at the bedside of a terminally ill patient, my opinions hardly hold much water concerning life and death issues. When a person is teetering between life and death, the only real comfort available is an objective word of truth that insures the inevitable loss of life will mean a new beginning and not the end. The fear of death can hardly be alleviated by man's assurances since the one dying knows all too well that man speaks from inexperience about the unknown. When God speaks, that is a different matter. God speaks from the vantage point of being above it all. God knows all, creates all, and in Christ has defeated death for those who place their faith in him.

Every person and every church, as well as every religion, has strong opinions about truth. One is as good as another from a human vantage point, unless there is provided an objective revelation of truth standing apart from man's surmises. Jesus referred to himself as truth incarnate.[8] Any and all no-nonsense Christian ministries are grounded in the objective revelation of Christ we call the Bible. Period! All sources of Christian teaching derive their authority from the revealed Word of our God.[9] Furthermore, because the message that the ministries of our Savior proclaim is God's Word, then it is entirely trustworthy and true.[10] How can it be otherwise? If God's Word is unreliable then objective truth is unknown and mankind is left alone with subjective truth. This appears to be the conclusion of many Christians and the churches they represent.

If we depend upon subjective truth to guide us then one man's truth is as good as another. And we are all groping in the dark hoping to discover the light. The church celebrates that the light of truth has been revealed. "All Scripture is God breathed and is useful for teaching, rebuking, correcting and training in righteousness, so that the man of God may be thoroughly equipped for every good work."[11]

No-nonsense ministries derive their authority from this divine revelation of truth and from nothing else.

There definitely exists a great division between Christians who hold to all of the Bible as the authoritative Word of the living God and those who hold to only certain theological concepts embedded in the Bible. Within both camps are divisions concerning how one properly interprets and understands this supernatural authority. My aim is not to enter into the specifics of those debates or sort through the entrapments that exist for extremists on any side. I do seek to make clear one truth – the Christian Church exists and exercises teaching authority *only* because of revealed truth that lies outside of man's ability to discern. Natural knowledge is not capable of bringing us into personal contact and recognition of God as our Redeemer.

No-nonsense ministry is not grounded in a *potential* connectedness to the Word of God. Nor is such ministry grounded in the social agendas of the day. No-nonsense ministries are not grounded in faddish experiences that throw traditions out the window. Neither are no-nonsense ministries grounded in the traditions of man, as fine as those traditions may be. The no-nonsense church is grounded in the Word of God. As all confessional writings, creedal statements or church hymnody should reflect the truth of Scripture, so also all decisions, attitudes, mission or vision statements must be securely founded upon the truth of God's Word. Only the rock of Jesus Christ provides a proper foundation for the church.

Churches representing Jesus Christ have become perverted reflections of God's revealed truth whenever they stray from the Word towards self-made authorities with self-created agendas. The flesh is incapable of coming to the truth or understanding it.[12] Led by the flesh, anything may seem right, anything may be taught, and all things become sheer nonsense. In the absence of the Spirit of Christ, the mind of man twists and perverts the Word of God to satisfy the cravings of the flesh.[13]

Scientists, historians and academic intellectuals may dance in the shadow of truth, but to know the truth one must sit at the feet of the Creator and listen. The world may obtain a glimpse of the truth in the reflections of creation, but the central truth upon which God's people build their lives is only obtainable as a gift from God, and therefore originates outside of man's observations and consequential conclusions. Man's total dependency upon the Maker for truth creates the church's agenda.

The no-nonsense church is grounded in the feeding upon God's Word.[14] This dependency upon what God is sowing involves the entire scope of ministry. To be grounded in the Word is not merely an intellectual exercise. More is involved than oversight of doctrinal purity. A congregation may insure that all of the doctrinal t's are crossed and i's are dotted by utilizing only approved hymnbooks and resources, but immaculate doctrinal oversight will be a great blessing only as members actually feed upon the Word revealed.

Worship traditions may accentuate and underscore a true confession of the faith, but if the steps of ritualism lull worshippers asleep, then presentation has become a trap for blindness.[15] No-nonsense churches recognize the need for a fresh and pure proclamation of God's Word. They also remain ever in touch with man's habitual need to add or subtract to God's authoritative Word. Only when the ministry is grounded in the Word will a church discern teachings that are not tainted by the false.[16]

The no-nonsense church clings steadfast to the Gospel of Christ as the power of God unto salvation.[17] No-nonsense ministries are ever concerned with the retention of the truth. By refusing to interpret Scripture out of context, they are engaged in letting Scripture speak for itself. Never satisfied to simply celebrate the rejection of falsehood in days gone by, God's people carry a living concern in the present to recognize and reject whatever opposes the revelation of God, even if such opposition has a long standing history. Any understanding of truth that is not verified by Scripture remains suspect as a product of the flesh.

The Spirit of God is given for guidance into the truth?[18] The flesh repeatedly sabotages the Spirit's counsel. The flesh is too apt to stray from the revealed Word of God, even reinventing truth in its own likeness. The flesh, the world, and Satan bombard Christians with temptations to discount what God has said. Christians regularly seek justification for denying the truth by declaring, "I know the Bible says, but...." Following the "but" is an entire discourse on why they cannot accept what Scripture teaches about an issue. "Do you believe that the Bible is God's Word?" I inquire. The answer is usually given in the affirmative. "Then, I do not understand," I reply. "How can you acknowledge the Bible as God's Word but then disagree with God? Do you really believe that you know better than God what is true and right?" I ask.

No-nonsense ministries are instruments of God, providing a setting that enables the building up of one another in the most holy faith.[19] Growing in the faith requires God's people to arrange their lives around the study of Scriptures. In this way, the no-nonsense church is able to test the spirits.[20] God's people actively engage in Bible study as a means of remaining faithful to the Lord. The study of God's Word happens in a wide variety of opportunities and settings. The church prioritizes the Word in all of her ministry activities.

The majority of Christians, unfortunately, remain unfamiliar with the Bible's actual teachings. Basing much of their belief on what is communicated through feelings, books and media; far too many Christians develop an unbiblical concept of truth. Nonsense occurs when Christians are Biblically illiterate or disengaged from a personal study of God's Word.

In striving to be good stewards of her resources, the no-nonsense church seeks to provide the opportunity for every member to gather around the study of the Bible. A greater value is placed upon hearing God's Word than any other activity. Bible studies and Sunday School may not have been prominent in the 16th century when sermons involved over an hour of Biblical expository preaching, but today's 15-20 minute weekly sermon will not suffice for one's entire diet of the Word.

Why, then, is the study of God's Word treated as an optional activity among God's people? Why are so many bored with what God has to say? Why do congregations promote the lack of interest in Biblical studies by their failure to prioritize Bible class opportunities? Churches promote the optional treatment of Bible study by the way they downplay Biblical study expectations. The financial choices the congregation makes also reveals a low priority placed on the study of God's Word. Since the Word is the means by which God works His grace in our lives, the church ought to view Bible study as a necessity for all Christians?

We treat the works of faith as necessary while we neglect the very means by which God works faith and its fruit. At other times we treat the Word as a vehicle to clean up our outward appearances while sabotaging the penetrating effect on our inner cleansing. Unless the Word is allowed to enter the deepest recesses of the heart, a Pharisaic change is insured.

I place a challenge before the membership over which I serve as pastor. If any member can only identify one hour, beyond worship, to give in service to the church, then my direction is to give the hour in one of our Bible fellowship studies.[21] I discourage anyone from serving in any other capacity in our congregation unless they give their first fruits of time in the study of God's Word. Any member who is attempting to serve in the "business" of the church without continually reflecting upon the Word of God will not have the wisdom, discernment, motivation, energy or passion to serve God's agenda among us.

Some churches may require every member to be connected with a small group, viewing themselves as a "church of small groups." Great! As long as those groups are engaged in the study of God's Word, in addition to the fellowship and prayer activities of the group. In no-nonsense ministries, members pledge themselves to remain students of the Word, understanding the purpose for which God gave pastors and teachers to the fellowship of believers.[22]

No-nonsense ministries also understand that to remain grounded in the Word her professional ministers must be apt to teach.[23] The church's spiritual leaders must not be unfamiliar with Biblical truth. Any leader in the church who is Biblically illiterate brings nonsense to the church's mission. No-nonsense ministry teams solicit students of the Word. Responsible lay leaders are solicited from the pool of members engaged in Bible Study. Nothing less is expected of all disciples of Christ than that they hunger for the truth of God and are regularly feeding upon his Word.[24]

All decisions, all priorities, all activities are viewed under the microscope of God's revealed truth. Nothing escapes the attention of the Word. Since resources are limited, the emphasis on the study of the Word receives utmost priority in all areas of ministry. The disruption of Bible study is rarely entertained for any reason.

The no-nonsense church operates around a three-fold emphasis: "be in the Word, on your knees, and looking beyond yourself!" The emphasis on the first imperative expresses the impetus and power for the other two. Prayer and the service of others flow continuously in response to God's Word imbedded in the heart.

Digging deeper into God's living Word enables the recipient to understand what the good and gracious will of our Heavenly Father is for his children on earth.[25] Regular students of the Word welcome the truth of God into their painful miseries and disappointments of life. In this way, they effectively battle the temptation to develop a life of pretense.

Satan's continual attack upon the Bible does not surprise the church that understands the purpose of the Holy Scriptures. John proclaimed; "These are written that you may believe that Jesus is the Christ, the Son of God, and that by believing you may have life in his name?"[26] The instigator of death is bent on destroying life. The early church experienced multiple attempts from outside forces to wipe out Christianity and the Bible. God brought relief in the conversion of the Roman emperor, Constantine. When outside forces were not successful, Satan found a foothold from within the church and accomplished having the Scriptures removed from God's people during most of the dark ages of history.

Once again our gracious God made a countermove and brought relief through Martin Luther and other reformers in the 16th century reformation of the church. Through these reformers, God called the church back to "sola scriptura" (Scripture alone) for the authority of all she preaches and teaches. The battle continued. In the 19th century there arose an intellectualism that discounted, disputed, and attempted to destroy the integrity of God's Word. In the post-modern era, the teachings of the Bible continue to be ridiculed, ignored, and mocked by a vast number of those who claim allegiance to Christ.

God warned that there would be those who hold to the form of religion while rejecting the truth. "But mark this: There will be terrible times in the last days. People will be lovers of themselves, lovers of money, boastful, proud, abusive, disobedient to their parents, ungrateful, unholy, without love, unforgiving, slanderous, without self-control, brutal, not lovers of the good, treacherous, rash, conceited, lovers of pleasure rather than lovers of God – having a form of godliness but denying its powers. Have nothing to do with them.[27]

That day has surely arrived. We may primarily observe it by the increasing number of Christians who embrace the "Good Book," but discount the Bible's teachings. The day of absurdity has arrived! Man has, from the beginning, been tempted to view himself as higher in intelligence than his Maker by questioning the authority of God's Word.[28] Today such arrogance is the mark of "higher learning." Man is approaching the point of no return in his defiance of God's Word.

Christ said, "Heaven and earth will pass away, but my words will never pass away."[29] In the end, obstinate rejection of the truth will bring forth the wrath of the Lamb who gave his life so man might live.[30] Christ warned against adding to or subtracting from the Word given to his people.[31] The end of man's profanity against the Lamb will not be pretty. Mankind blindly elevates itself for destruction.[32]

Scripture warns, "But there were also false prophets among the people, just as there will be false teachers among you. They will secretly introduce destructive heresies, even denying the sovereign Lord who bought them – bringing swift destruction on themselves. Many will follow their shameful ways and will bring the way of truth into disrepute. In their greed, these teachers will exploit you with stories they have made up. Their condemnation has long been hanging over them, and their destruction has not been sleeping."[33]

No-nonsense ministries are united in their recognition that the church's real battle is not against flesh and blood, but against the powers of darkness.[34] Strip the church of God's Word and you have left only the teachings of men corrupted by the flesh. Keep the Word, but strip it of meaning and power and you have the fruits of liberalism or dead orthodoxy. These theological positions may appear to travel in the direction of truth, but in actuality they have taken a detour. Only the church engaged in nonsense fails to discern what's at stake in calling the integrity of God's Word into question.

The no-nonsense church works to equip every member with the Word of God. "Your word is a lamp to my feet and a light for my path."[35] No-nonsense leaders understand their role as equippers.[36] They also understand that the first and primary goal in equipping the saints is proclaiming/teaching the Word of God.[37] Through Biblical exhortations, the Spirit of God works to create faith in the hearts of the hearers and fruit in the lives of the recipients.[38]

No-nonsense ministries do not deviate from this priority of ministry. Nor do her pastors relinquish this priority. They may share the task of teaching the Word with others who are gifted by God to do so, but pastors do not excuse themselves from teaching the Word by relinquishing the task to others.[39] In no-nonsense ministry the spiritual leaders delegate the necessary business matters in order that they may focus attention upon the ministry of the Word of God.[40]

Where is the hunger for feeding upon the Word of God? There are indeed those congregations who stress the need for God's people to be in the Word. Thank you God! A more significant number of churches, in every community, place little emphasis on providing Bible study opportunities. What has robbed the church of her passion for God's Word? Statistics provide discouraging evidence of how few Christians are really committed to learning the truths of God. Even in those congregations whereby the study of God's Word is prioritized, only a small percentage of the overall worship population actually participates in a Bible study. Why are God's people consistently neglectful of this life giving food? Jesus proclaimed, "Man does not live on bread alone, but on every word that comes from the mouth of God."[41]

The no-nonsense church recognizes that the heart of the matter lies in the flesh's opposition to the Spirit. The church aims to supply the food necessary for her members to effectively battle the flesh. The no-nonsense church is relentless in intensifying the call for all Christians to become diligent students of the Word. And she prioritizes her resources to insure that opportunities abound for her members to mature in their understanding of the Word.

Many congregations have opted to discontinue the Sunday morning Bible class in order to make way for an additional worship service. Space is the ongoing concern. Is eliminating the hour of Bible study for adults the best answer to the problem of space? Many of these same churches offer worship and Sunday School concurrently, causing parents and children to part ways when entering the church. As a result, parents do not attend study and children never attend worship.

The limitations and struggles of a growing church produce few easy answers. Thankful for the growth, congregations often cave in to the easiest of solutions. Whatever solutions the church presents in dealing with space and financial limitations, the no-nonsense church remains convicted that engaging in a life long study of God's Word is imperative to a growing and mature faith in Christ.

Churches that opt to eliminate a Bible class, in order to offer an additional worship service, usually cut the pastor's class from the schedule. This is extremely unfortunate. Usually, the pastor is the highest trained in Biblical teachings. The pastor may not be the most gifted to teach, but rarely are layman more trained. The primary task of the pastoral office is communicating the truth of Scriptures. All pastors, regardless of their specified roles, ought to be first and foremost conveyors of the Word of God in word and deed. This may be accomplished in multiple settings. From the pulpit to the classroom, in the counseling session and the home visit, pastors ought to be engaged in the continual teaching of God's Word. Woe to the church whereby her pastor/s no longer prioritize such work.

Small group ministries have provided a wonderful setting whereby ten or so Christians gather around the study of God's Word to learn, pray and share their lives together. Structuring the life of the congregation around small group Bible study is an excellent recognition that the Body depends upon the spiritual food that God has supplied, in order to experience true community and fulfill her mission. Satan, in cahoots with the flesh, continually seeks entrance into such groups in order to sabotage their purpose. All such groups ought to be on constant guard against forming closed cliques, using prayer and sharing time as seedbeds for gossip and slander, or losing sight of the purpose and mission of the church.

No-nonsense ministries are ever concerned with the retention of the truth.[42] They take seriously the many Scriptural warnings of being deceived and led down the path of falsehood.[43] The fight of faith ever perseveres against the false and the flesh.[44] The no-nonsense church remains balanced in her presentation of the Law and Gospel teachings of Scripture because she remains grounded in the Word. When the church's teachings are thrown off balance by confusing the Law with the Gospel then either legalistic or libertine tendencies result.[45]

The no-nonsense congregation realizes how narrow the path to eternal life.[46] With the flesh beckoning the spirit away from the truth and the world shouting it's amen, only the Spirit of God working through the message of Christ insures the path that is straight. Those who stray off the straight and narrow path of life fall into ditches on either side. Stuck in a ditch the ministry may appear very zealous in its overemphasis of some aspect of the truth, while disregarding or even denying another aspect. Traveling in the ditch one is vulnerable to the run offs of the world where mud and garbage collect.

Ministries may become very complacent in defending their ditch positions. Spending more time defending the ditch then traveling down the path laid out for her, such ministries spin their wheels in nonsense. Even worse, a church's blindness to the truth may result in her condemnation of those who are actually traveling the path of God's plan.[47] Like teenagers, hiding out in ditches waiting to throw stones at passing cars, ministries often become fixated on stoning the prophets sent to them.[48]

No-nonsense churches are never interested in laying aside the Word of God in order to appeal to the masses or the seeker.[49] Churches ought to be interested in designing innovative settings by which unbelievers might give ear to the message of truth in Christ. God's people are to bring the Gospel to the lost and they must speak the language unbelievers can understand in order to do so.[50] However, that language must speak the truth.

The no-nonsense church does not pretend to be something she is not. Nor do no-nonsense ministries water down the truth of God or side step it. They resist the temptation to compromise the truth in order to share the message of Christ. Christ embodies the truth and any presentation of Christ strives to convey the whole truth connected to Christ. Apart from Christ there is no truth for he himself is the embodiment of truth.[51]

The no-nonsense church understands the difficulties in remaining true to the Word of God. Totally dependent upon God for the Word, she also understands her total dependence upon the Spirit for understanding the Word. No-nonsense ministries always approach the

Word in sincere humility, expecting to be taught, enlightened, and clarified in the truth.

No-nonsense Christians realize that they are apt to stray, and therefore they anticipate and welcome correction. They are faithful students of the Word. They incorporate prayer as a discipline surrounding the study of God's Word. Nothing less expresses the total dependency upon God to provide understanding of the truth. The Sword of the Spirit is absolutely essential for members of the Body of Christ to stand against the attacks of Satan.[52]

The no-nonsense church has learned the art of listening and the necessity of sitting at the feet of the Creator. The ministry is patterned after Mary, rather than Martha.[53] In the priority of hearing the Word, the worship setting takes on tremendous importance. No-nonsense ministries are ever evaluating worship settings with an eye on the clarity of God's Word presented. They continually analyze the dynamics of sight and sound as it affects the effectiveness of "hearing." Striving to remove as many obstacles and distractions as possible to enhance worshippers in becoming recipients of the Word, no-nonsense leaders utilize God's blessings to insure the best setting for receiving the message of God. Apathy or indifference towards the presentation of God's Word, whereby the ministry places less then her best foot forward, is not allowed.

Kingdom work in Christ must begin with the intentional listening to the Word of God. When God's people bypass the power source of service, then they discover that their efforts are at best hit and miss endeavors. The church that fails to plug into the power source of God experiences a continual work force of volunteers, who are burned-out, embittered, confused, discouraged, and distracted servants.

Christians, who begin their service in the fellowship of the Word, discover a reservoir of time, talents and treasures not previously discerned. In actuality, the Spirit working through the Word of God has renewed the spirit, transformed the mind and changed the heart of the hearer. With renewed passion and energy, a growing vision emerges within the soul of the servant that develops the character of perseverance in the truth. As Jesus says, "He who has an ear, let him hear what the Spirit says to the churches."[54]

One of the most challenging endeavors in the Christian Church consists of the weekly sermon. The pastoral task of presenting the Word of God in a relevant, applicable, and vibrant delivery, week after week, to all ages of diverse educational and economic levels, while not becoming overly repetitive or boring, sobers the servant of God. The difficulty of the task is especially recognized when one considers the 21st century attention span.

Technology has created an expectation of the dramatic, visual and sound effects, that play on the emotions. Technology has indeed given us many new and positive tools for preaching and teaching in the church, but not without raising the bar of apparent excellence by redefining the delivery that is acceptable. Just as our children are losing the art of imagination as they turn away from the reading of books towards media fascination, likewise, all of us find ourselves growing more impatient with simply listening to expository preaching.

This is the cultural reality with which no-nonsense ministries must contend in reaching individuals within the context of today's world. The no-nonsense church prays to be used as God's instrument of change in people's lives. Regardless of the setting, change will occur only through the faithful presentation of God's Word.[55] This is, without doubt, what led Abraham Lincoln to conclude that the Bible was the best gift God has given to man. Actually, the Bible is the means by which the greatest gift is given, namely, the living Word of God – Jesus Christ. The presentation of the gift of God's Son is the overriding goal of ministry. The no-nonsense church is determined to share God's Word with others that they may not only know Christ, but also know what is the good and acceptable will of God.

Now is the time for the ministries of the Incarnate Word to let his light shine in the darkness of this world.[56] Only the truth of Christ offers freedom from enslavement to the flesh.[57] There are many who seek to lead God's people away from the truth of Christ.[58] No-nonsense ministries celebrate that the Word of God IS the truth.[59] And the truth received is the truth shared. The love of Christ compels his people to bond together in voicing the truth to the "now" generation searching for God.

Digging Deeper into the Word of God

1. Read Colossians 3:16. Does the Word of Christ include all of Scripture, Old and New Testaments, prophetic and apostolic, or does it merely include the message of John 3:16?

2. Read 1 Peter 1:23-25. If the teachings of the Bible are truly the imperishable word of God, then how ought we to treat them? Does our congregation prioritize the study of God's Word? How is our church encouraging an every member study of the Bible? What percentage of our congregation's total membership is identified as members of a Bible class?

3. Read 2 Peter 1:16-21. Peter taught that the Old Testament prophecies pointed to Christ. The word of the prophets of old were made more certain by the salvation brought by the Messiah, Jesus Christ. The message was no invention of man, but inspired by the Spirit of God. In light of this, how does your congregation insure that all members are ongoing students of God's Word?

4. Read Mark 1:1-20 (cf. Matthew 13:1-23; Luke 8:4-15). What does this parable teach God's people about the word of God? What are the warnings embedded in this parable concerning the receiving of God's Word? What does it mean for someone to accept the word after hearing it so that a bountiful crop is produced? Is your church vigorously involved in such active hearing? What tends to sabotage attendance at your congregation's Bible class opportunities?

5. Read John 20:30-31. John expresses that his purpose for writing is that his readers may believe in Jesus Christ and receive true life. If the word is viewed as the instrument, the vehicle, or the means by which God's Spirit brings a sinner to repentance and faith, then how does this conviction effect your congregation's ministry decisions? If a person evaluated your church's financial statement would they be able to affirm that the hearing of God's Word is a priority? Read Isaiah 55:10-11; Romans 1:16, 10:16-18; 1 Corinthians 12:3; Ephesians 5:25-27, 1 Thessalonians 2:13

and James 1:18. Reflect on the importance of the Word of God in the ministry of Jesus Christ.

6. Memorize 2 Timothy 3:16-17; "All Scripture is God-breathed and is useful for teaching, rebuking, correcting and training in righteousness, so that the man of God may be thoroughly equipped for every good work."

Endnotes

[1] Mark 9:7

[2] Revelation 1:12-18

[3] The original was written by Dean E. Feldmeyer, who is also credited for the ingenious originality embedded in the association of the big bad wolf with "The Way Life Is."

[4] 1 Corinthians 10:23

[5] 2 Timothy 3:5

[6] Matthew 7:24-27

[7] For more information on this subject, see "What's a Worldview Anyway?" by Del Tackett. July/August 2004 issue of Focus on the Family magazine pp 7-9, Copyright © 2004, Focus on the Family. This nation-wide survey determined that only 4 percent of Americans had a "biblical" worldview.

[8] John 14:6

[9] 2 Peter 1:20-21 (cf. Matthew 28:18-20; specifically our Lord's command to teach everything He has commanded.)

[10] 2 Samuel 22:31, Proverbs 30:5, and Psalm 12:6

[11] 2 Timothy 3:16

[12] Romans 8:7-8

[13] cults, Jim Jones, Charles Manson, David Koresch are prime examples of perverting the Word of God

[14] Deuteronomy 8:3 (cf. the temptation of Jesus in Matthew 4:4 and Luke 4:4)

[15] Matthew 15:6

[16] Hebrews 4:12

[17] Romans 1:16

[18] John 14:26 and John 16:13a

[19] 1 Thessalonians 5:11

[20] 1 John 4:1 (cf. 1 Thessalonians 5:21)

[21]The failure to identify any additional time to do the Lord's work beyond Bible study is absurd.

[22]Ephesians 4:11-12

[23]2 Timothy 2:24 and 4:2

[24]Colossians 3:16

[25]Ephesians 5:17

[26]John 20:31

[27]2 Timothy 3:1-5

[28]Genesis 3; the original temptation into sin revolved around the question of whether what God had commanded was really in the best interest of man

[29]Matthew 24:35

[30]Revelation 3:3

[31]Revelation 22:19

[32]Revelation 11:18

[33]2 Peter 2:1-3

[34]Ephesians 6:12

[35]Psalm 119:105 (cf. Psalm 119:9, 11, 103, 130, 160)

[36]2 Timothy 3:17

[37]Romans 10:14-15

[38]Romans 10:17 (cf. 1 Corinthians 12:3 and Ephesians 5:26)

[39]2 Timothy 2:15

[40]Acts 6:2

[41]Matthew 4:4

[42]John 15:7

[43]Titus 3:3 (cf. 2 Timothy 3:13)

[44]1 Timothy 1:18-19 (cf. 6:12)

[45]Romans chapters 3-8 are excellent Biblical references for distinguishing between the Law and Gospel

[46]Matthew 7:13-14

[47]Mark 9:38-40

[48]Matthew 23:37

[49]2 Corinthians 2:17 and 4:2

[50]1 Corinthians 14:19

[51]John 14:6

[52]Ephesians 6:14 and 6:17-18

[53]Luke 10:38-42

[54]Revelation 2:7

[55]Isaiah 55:11
[56]2 Peter 1:19-21
[57]John 8:32, 36, (cf. Psalm 146:7)
[58]2 Timothy 4:3-4
[59]John 17:17

Chapter 3 - Spirit Empowered
(or "How Did We Stray This Far?")

"Not by might nor by power,
but by my Spirit, says the Lord Almighty."
Zechariah 4:6b

Adventurous Kathy wanted to go exploring on the Wisconsin farm with her older cousin, Liz. As they walked toward the fields where the old barn stood, they discovered a narrow path. So narrow that the two could not walk side by side, but one had to follow the other. On the left was a loosely hung strand of barbed wire, held up by a few flimsy sticks of wood. On the right was an open field of tall grass.

The two followed this path a good distance before realizing that the field on the left was actually a bullpen. A heard of bulls began charging toward them, gathering to the strand of wire. Mere inches away from them, the bulls, en masse, kept step with the girls.

The older and wiser Liz knew that they were in great danger. Slowly, she squatted down and urged her younger loved one onto her shoulders. Kathy could see the large wild eyes that watched her every move. She pleaded with her cousin to put her down so that she could run away.

Liz whispered gently, "no." Kathy could feel the firm grip of Liz's hands on her legs. Liz turned around and began a slow trek back. "Just let me down and I promise I will not run," Kathy pleaded. The promise was insincere and Liz knew it. No amount of manipulating pleads would cause Kathy's cousin to set her free. Liz just quietly sang hymns as she slowly carried Kathy to safety.

My wife, Kathy, was only seven years old when she learned the lesson well that her way was not always the best way. When faced with danger our fear prompts us to get out the bargaining chips and make all sorts of promises that we never plan to keep. When the perceived danger subsides we usually return to the way life was before the panic button was pushed. Christians follow God down the narrow path of life. Everything is well until danger reveals itself. God appears stubborn in his refusal to heed our promises and bless our plans. The more we fear the danger of failure in our ministry's efforts the more we intensify our control of the situation. God patiently quiets our fears as He carries us to safer pastures.

The no-nonsense church is empowered by the Spirit of God. In the Spirit, Christians are able to settle their fears by trusting in God's promises to supply what the ministry really needs. Only then do God's people discern the blessing of not receiving everything for which they have asked. God often withholds immediate provisions in order to root out the fears that create panicky requests. The Spirit digs deep in order to get at the heart of the matter. The no-nonsense church rejoices that God is always working for the good of those who love him, even when their plans fail.

The Christian Church should not find it difficult to discern the Spirit's presence and power when Christ remains center-stage. His Word shines the light for our earthly journey.[1] What if God had left us in the dark? When a church becomes bogged down with the heavy-laden affairs of the world and the cares of the flesh, then the Spirit of God is quenched.

The church can predict what will follow when members become self-absorbed instead of enamored by her Lord. Selfish attitudes, decisions, and behaviors increase and division, jealousy, gossip and slander become an integral part of her identity. When Satan is given an open door, then the spirit of the anti-Christ prevails until Christ is once again invited to take center-stage.

I am a music lover. Music moves my soul in a way that nothing else seems to do. From Handle's "Hallelujah Chorus," to the hymn, "Beautiful Savior," music inspires me to lift my praises on high.

Many contemporary songs move my spirit as well, redirecting my focus away from the world of nonsense towards Christ and his Word. The late Rich Mullin's song, "If I Stand," never ceases to move my soul to reaffirm my life embedded in the grace of Christ. Secular songs may also solicit within me certain feelings of love, sadness, joy, commitment and nostalgia. Martin Luther noted the great value of music. He once expressed that, except for theology, no art was equal to music.

The point of the church's engagement with music has to do with the Word of our God. The Body of Christ guards against being deceived into equating emotional highs and lows with the Spirit's presence. In the worship setting, words put to music are Biblically accurate. Lyrics that fail to convey the truth of God ought to be excluded from the worship of God's people. We are confident of the Spirit's presence, guidance and gifts entirely because of God's Word conveyed, whether in the context of music, preaching, teaching or symbols.

The no-nonsense church is Spirit empowered precisely because she is Christ-centered and Word grounded. The people of God may debate on the specific gifts of the Holy Spirit operating in the church, but there should be no debate on the Scriptural truth that the Spirit's presence is an absolute necessity; not a peripheral addendum in the life of the fellowship of believers. He is the Spirit of the living Christ in all who genuinely confess Jesus as Savior.[2]

Because the Spirit's presence is essential to the life of the church, no-nonsense ministries are deeply entrenched in Biblical study. The Word of God is the means by which the Spirit brings to God's people the grace and blessings of Christ.[3] Dependent upon God, no-nonsense ministries will always prioritize the means of the Spirit that convey the presence of her Lord.

By God's design, the acts of Baptism and the Lord's Supper are attached to the commands and promises of God's Word in Christ. The sacred act of God towards helpless sinners, in the sending of the Spirit and bringing individuals to repentant faith, is consistently linked in Scripture to the waters of Baptism. God's work of bonding his people in the forgiving love of Christ, sustaining true faith, and affirming the forgiveness of sins are intimately linked to the celebration of the Lord's Supper.

These acts, instituted and commanded by Christ, are not by-products in the life of the church, even though there exists a great division concerning the proper understanding and administration of Baptism and the Lord's Supper. Christians remain divided on whether these acts, commanded by Christ, are sacraments in which God works his grace or merely responses to the work of his grace. Christians are further divided on the appropriate fellowship and administration of these actions. Such division continues to be a sad, but true, reality in the church since the 16th century Reformation. The aim of this book is not to enter this very important debate among Christians or bring resolution to the divisions. There are many excellent resources expounding on the Biblical teachings in this regard.

The point underscored here is that what God commands and associates with his work of grace are not peripheral issues in the Body of Christ. God's means of communicating his work of grace through the Word of life in Christ do not lie on the fringes of the Spirit's presence. Since no-nonsense ministries are grounded in the Word of God they do not lay aside what God elevates as important activities in the life of his people.

The importance of Baptism is clearly expressed in the great commission of our Lord and commanded in the making of disciples.[4] Baptism is closely linked with the possession of true faith in Christ.[5] Matthew, Mark, and Luke, in recording the institution of the Lord's Supper by Christ, in addition to Paul's account, underscore the importance of this divine meal.[6] Further importance is underscored by Paul's strictest warnings given to those who abuse the celebration or receive it unprepared.[7]

These public actions, administered by the fellowship of God's people in the Body of Christ, do not originate in man's traditions or ideas. They express God's will for his people. No-nonsense ministries do not have a disregard for that which Christ has instituted. When Baptism and the Lord's Supper are treated as unimportant or irrelevant to the worship and life of God's people, then the ministry, grounded in the Word of God, has communicated confusion. This confusion is nonsense.

Without the Spirit of God the church ends up presenting a lifeless orthodox dogma or a meaningless emotional obsession with feeling.

Jesus taught, "Unless I go away, the Counselor will not come to you; but if I go, I will send him to you. When he comes, he will convict the world of guilt in regard to sin and righteousness and judgment: in regard to sin, because men do not believe in me; in regard to righteousness, because I am going to the Father, where you can see me no longer; and in regard to judgment, because the prince of this world now stands condemned."[8]

The Spirit of God descends as God determines. Jesus compared the Spirit of God with the wind. He said, "The wind blows wherever it pleases. You hear its sound, but you cannot tell where it comes from or where it is going. So it is with everyone born of the Spirit."[9] The Spirit of God comes as God has promised. The Lord Almighty has linked the outpouring of his Spirit with the giving of his Word and the confession of Jesus Christ.

The Holy Spirit enables the faith of God's people.[10] The Spirit of God keeps the church focused. No true member of the Body of Christ is without the Spirit of Christ.[11] The presence of the Spirit of the living God enables the church to keep her eyes on Jesus. All of the gifts of the Spirit operating in the Body has but one aim; namely, to keep God's people in the saving confession of Jesus as Lord and Savior. The no-nonsense church understands this essential reality.

The ministry of Christ arises from, depends upon, and is sustained by the power and presence of the Holy Spirit. When the Spirit is quenched, or worst, rejected, then the flame of faith flickers and is threatened by extinguishment. Paul instructs, "Do not put out the Spirit's fire."[12] This command is preceded by commands for God's people to "be joyful always; pray continually; give thanks in all circumstances, for this is God's will for you in Christ Jesus."[13] And immediately following the exhortation to not put out the Spirit's fire, Paul commands, "Do not treat prophecies with contempt. Test everything. Hold on to the good. Avoid every kind of evil."[14]

God commands his people to "be filled with the Spirit."[15] To be filled with the Spirit is to engage in activities of the Spirit. The Spirit remains aflame in ministries grounded in the truth of God's Word whose response incorporates prayer, praise and thanksgiving. In commanding the filling of the Spirit, Paul further instructs, "Speak to one another with psalms, hymns, and spiritual songs. Sing and make music in your heart to the Lord, always giving thanks to God the Father for everything, in the name of our Lord Jesus Christ."[16] Prayer, praise and thanksgiving are Spirit-empowered responses on the part of God's children.

Void of the Spirit of God there would be no faith and without faith there would be no life. The purpose of the Spirit is to bring glory to God the Father by lifting up his Son, Jesus Christ, in the eyes and hearts of people. Christ is the object of the Spirit's work. Just as all spiritual gifts point to the Savior, so also, all gifts of the Spirit serve the common good of the Body.[17] All gifts aim at the maturity and growth of the Body in the faith and obedience of Christ.[18] The fruit of the Spirit bond the children of the Heavenly Father together in their worship of Christ.

The highlight of the fellowship of believers lies in her worship of God. Worship involves, first and foremost, the feeding upon the Bread of Life. Worship also includes the Spirit prompted responses of God's people through the confessions of sin and faith, along with prayers and petitions. Gifts of time, talents, and treasures are offered in service to the Lord. Worship is exemplary of the relationship that God has established in Christ with those who believe. Any meaningful relationship involves initiation and response. Worship is divided between the receiving and returning, the listening and responding, expressions of a personal relationship with the Almighty God. In worship, God gives himself that we might give in return.

The church that enters worship in the spirit of arrogance quenches the presence of God's Spirit. To worship in spirit and truth expresses the sincere humility of poor sinners who have been gifted with genuine faith. Unlike the Pharisee who arrogantly stood before God, beating his brow in false pride, true worshippers prostrate their souls before their Maker Redeemer in repentance and faith.[19] The hearts of those gathered in no-nonsense worship never lose sight of the "amazing grace that saved a wretch like me."[20]

The worship of God's people promotes "self-examination." Confessional declarations of sin and faith call to the worshipper's attention the answers to two important questions: 1. Do I sincerely acknowledge and repent of my sins? And 2. Do I genuinely believe/ trust in Jesus Christ as my Savior from sin? A third question serves to test the integrity of repentance and faith; namely, 3. Do I intend to amend my sinful ways? The call to faith in Christ is a call away from sin for service. Repentance always involves acknowledgement and recognition of personal sin.

With their eyes glued upon Jesus and grounded in his teachings, God's people live within the boundaries that God has set forth, in order that they may reach their best in Christ. The toleration of willful disobedience in the church's fellowship is detrimental to the body/soul/spirit welfare of believers. If the sin that so easily entangles our families is ignored, then we experience the brokenness of relationships. When individual families are broken then the greater family is impaired.

The toleration of unrepentant sin in the home results in the destruction of harmony, peace, joy, faith, hope and love, in the church as well. When sin is not put in check by the Spirit's power then dissension, hatred, discord, malice, jealousy and bitterness results in broken and abused relationships, revealing the perversions of those bearing the name Christian. This observable reality is detestable to our God and destructive to his Body.[21]

The church engulfed in disobedience drives out the Holy Spirit from her midst by remaining apathetic to the rooted sin that attaches itself to the Body. Unconfessed sin is bound to grow and flourish if not crushed and destroyed through repentance and faith. As the Scriptures say, "If we claim to be without sin, we deceive ourselves and the truth is not in us. If we confess our sins, he is faithful and just and will forgive us our sins and purify us from all unrighteousness. If we claim we have not sinned, we make him out to be a liar and his word has no place in our lives."[22]

The Law of God is given for the primary purpose of exposing and condemning sin. Collectively, God's people are empowered by the Spirit of God to seek out and uproot any sin that entangles the flock. God's people must not turn a deaf ear to the sin that lives in their midst. Too much is at stake. It is a matter of life and death eternally.

Psalm one beautifully expresses this attitude of God's people, "Blessed is the man who does not walk in the counsel of the wicked or stand in the way of sinners or sit in the seat of mockers. But his delight is in the law of the Lord, and on his law he meditates day and night."[23] The purpose of the law given to man is not to provide a vehicle by which man can pass through the gates of heaven on his own merits. One's imperfect attempts to follow the law are surely not aimed at insuring or securing a place in God's Kingdom. The purpose is to open eyes to the reality of sin and bring recognition to the need for a Savior. Repentance is the work of the Spirit in preparation for opening the eyes of the heart to see Jesus as the Redeemer. This is God's work, as he not only prepares, but also creates and sustains true faith in the hearts and souls of the chosen.

Faith in Christ always involves contrition over sin. Unless the law serves its primary purpose of bringing a heart to the helpless condition of condemnation, the Gospel will not lift the soul from despair to hope. Until one weeps in sorrow over sin, he will not weep in joy over a Savior. When one is lifted by grace from his humbled position of helplessness, repentance becomes a way of life. As long as sin is present in the flesh to interfere with the work of God's Spirit, the contrite heart will remain a reality in the life of faith.

The work of God's Spirit is continually affirmed in the public acts, instituted by God, which identify his people with the defeat of sin. Baptism and the Lord's Supper serve as conveyors of the truth in Christ. Consequently, they also provide a public forum against sin. They are visible living realities of God's intolerance of sin, in that they are associated with and identified by the washing away of sin, brought by the presence of the sacrificial Lamb of God. And the point being made is that no-nonsense ministries are intricately involved with the call of God to repentance. Equipped with the stewardship of grace, the no-nonsense church calls people away from sin by inviting them to turn in faith to Christ.

When God's people become blinded to sin or worse yet, indifferent to sin, then the Spirit of God is quenched and Satan's power takes hold.[24] Paul warns against giving the devil a foothold.[25] Scripture conveys the boundaries involved in God-pleasing behavior. No-nonsense ministries realize that life in the Spirit is contrary to the desires of the sinful nature.

Flesh and spirit are ever pitted against each other in the Scriptures.[26] No-nonsense ministries are able to discern the presence of the Spirit by the fruit evident in the life of the fellowship.[27] Paul instructs those engaged in the ministry of the Lord, "Since we live by the Spirit, let us keep in step with the Spirit. Let us not become conceited, provoking and envying each other."[28]

Walking in the Spirit is hindered by the average Christian's attitude toward sin. Sin is typically categorized as simply breaking God's rules. God's law is often viewed completely separate from the boundaries of love. Rules disconnected to the relationships they serve become meaningless and pointless in the heart of the beholder. Christians find it difficult to weep over a traffic violation. Today's church too frequently squelches the daily need for contrition by undermining the Law of God. This happens whenever sin is treated lightly and viewed as irrelevant to God ordained relationships in the life of the Christian.

According to Christ, the one word that summed up perfect obedience to the Law of God was "love." Sin is therefore rightly viewed as love violations. When we understand that sinful disobedience is a gross rebellion against our relationship with God, and abuses our love for each other, then our hearts will weep in sorrow. The Lord taught his disciples to pray continually, "Forgive us our debts, as we also have forgiven our debtors."[29]

The increased relaxation of calling God's people into accountability is perplexing. The sin that runs rampant among unbelievers is not surprising. The failure on the part of the Body of Christ to separate herself from willful and intentional sin has provided impetus to the classic accusation of hypocrisy against members of the church.

A physician's daughter, formerly attending a Christian high school, now testifies to the hypocritical nature of the students there. "What hypocrites," she recalls, "drug use and sexual promiscuity is not any less active in the Christian high school then in the public school." What a sad commentary on Christian witness. Hypocrisy is the most popular reason many Christians advocate a private Christianity that is disconnected from any worshipping community. Needless to say, those who claim love for Christ and yet sever oneself from worship and service in his Body are engulfed in hypocrisy as well.

The sins of God's people understandably involve the same sins of the flesh as the rest of humanity; i.e. divorce, sexual immorality, gossip, slander, greed, selfishness, hatred and the like. This is not surprising. What is shocking is the immunity that has developed in the Church towards such unrepentant sins. Nothing quenches the Spirit like intentional willful sinning.

No-nonsense ministries recognize the need for rooting out sin in the fellowship of believers, for naming sin. Spirit empowered churches understand the distinction between repentant and unrepentant sinners. We are all sinners in need of forgiveness. Believers have been carried away by the Spirit of the living God into a heart of repentance and faith.

The no-nonsense church uses God's law in exercising admonition. Christ instructed the church to do so. Paul says, "Brothers, if someone is caught in a sin, you who are spiritual should restore him gently. But watch yourself, or you also may be tempted. Carry each other's burdens, and in this way you will fulfill the law of Christ."[30] Christ taught the same thing in Matthew.[31] The aim of church discipline is love. The goal is to win the brother back to the faith in the Lord Jesus Christ.[32]

As brothers and sisters in Christ, we seek the protection of those engaged in destructive decision-making and actions. The church empowered by the Spirit of God is a sober watchful church, watching out for each other through prayer and activated love. Spirit empowered ministries convey appropriate boundaries for the good of God's people. The no-nonsense church does not become immune to sin or lazy in obedience. The ministries of Jesus Christ do not equate forgiveness with toleration. Forgiveness is not a license to sin.[33]

Not only has divorce reached epidemic proportions in society, but divorce has also marched through the doors of our churches and rattled the sensibilities of God's people. Not that divorce is an unforgivable sin, but divorce often occurs in the Body without the slightest recognition that sin is involved. Whereas God says, "I hate divorce;"[34] God's people treat it as no big deal. Shall the people of God sweep the issue under the rug pretending that God is indifferent to the issue? The real absurdity is the presence of spiritual leaders who have obtained unscriptural divorces without any accountability to the Body.

Divorce is not the only blatant sin engaging the people of God. Living together without being married has risen in shocking numbers among those who are called by Christ to let his light shine. Sex without the bonds of holy matrimony has come out of the closet. And if the church provides testimony against the sin of such arrangements, couples will even lie to the pastor to hide what has become a public testimony to everyone else.

Christian parents vigorously defend their children's sinful living arrangements, while often condemning the pastor who brings such sin to light. Even if a couple is not living together out of wedlock, premarital sexual relationships are more common than not. Technically, not acceptable in most churches, such openly defiant and sinful behaviors among Christians often remain unchallenged by most churches. Forgiveness of sin continues to be equated with tolerance for sin, if the sin is recognized at all.

Sometimes forgiveness is viewed as not applicable because sin is no longer acknowledged as such. This is the case with homosexuality. John Kerry, a professed Catholic Christian, during the 2003 presidential debates, stated that God created some people to be homosexual. The tide has definitely turned away from the need to forgive to the need to accept and condone.

God creates all. All are sinners. But God does not create us to be sinners. Sin is derived from our original parents and continues to reside in our own flesh and hearts. Even if homosexuals are born with a propensity towards such, as others who are born with a propensity towards becoming alcoholics, the innate sinfulness of man does not undo God's declaration and condemnation of such behaviors as sinful in his sight. The Bible teaches we are born in sin and therefore each of us has a predisposition towards sin. Our individual uniqueness expresses the sinful nature in different ways, according to our individual weaknesses.

Every parent may observe how each child expresses differently this inclination toward sin. Some seem to be born with a tendency towards greed and selfishness, others towards arrogance, still others towards addictive behaviors. Some children seem to have a proclivity to lie from the moment they can talk; others have a penchant towards stealing or temper tantrums. If we are to embrace any behavior noticeable since birth as God ordained, then sin itself becomes a creation of God. Yet, the Bible makes it plain that we are all by nature objects of God's wrath.[35]

The same holds true for open and blatant immoral lifestyles of any sort.[36] Unacknowledged, unconfessed, unchecked sinful behaviors engage the church in dire consequences. Gossiping and slanderous behaviors are serious sins that quench the Spirit and destroy the fellowship of believers. Greed and poor stewardship practices are publicly flown in the church's face without any accountability required of those who engage in such sinful attitudes and lifestyles.

On and on the list could continue, revealing the church's perceived apathy to the destructive sins of her members. In today's society, with the constant exposure to sin and evil, all of us are quite aware of a growing mental exemption to wrongdoing. That is precisely why we need the Body of Christ to call us, each of us, into accountability, that no one may "lose what you have worked for, but that you may be rewarded fully."[37]

The Church of Jesus Christ persistently brings accountability, calling her members to "throw off everything that hinders and the sin that so easily entangles, and let us run with perseverance the race marked out for us."[38] Congregation's today are paying a heavy price for their willing participation in the world's insatiable appetite for sin. Sitting on the sidelines and remaining silent, the church should not be surprised that society sucks her members into its insanity. Television, movies, videos, games, and the World Wide Web have successfully brought inappropriate entertainment into our houses. Slowly God's people are seduced to ignore the ungodliness in which the world's entertainment is packaged.

The problem does not merely lie in the church's silence to satanic intrusions into our homes, but in the welcome mat that has been extended to the media by God's people as a whole. How are we to accept the reality that a nation of citizens claiming to trust in God willingly allows the onslaught of the vile without opposition? Many who claim the Christian identity pride themselves in watching the immorally degenerate and violent acts of man for their enjoyment. And churches stand by with a neglectful eye, promoting approval by the obvious absence of admonition.

Great confusion is evident among the churches of Christ concerning the expressed will of God for his people. The church that questions the authority or relevancy of the Bible compounds the confusion that exists. The intensity of Satan's penetration of evil into our homes will only increase as the battle for our souls heats up. Like the proverbial frog boiling in a kettle of water, because the temperature rises too slow for him to take notice, so God's people have allowed the polluted waters of the world to rise around them until the waters threaten to swallow them into a sea of madness.

How could the church have become so apathetic to the rising tide of evil? God warned the church to "keep oneself from being polluted by the world."[39] And now the church is called upon to fight, not just the pollution from without, but also the pollution from within. Wake up calls may be heard across the horizon. Listen carefully and you will hear the enemy's drums pounding as he intensifies his efforts within the walls of the church.

Confusion is further created by a misapplication of the often-quoted phrase, "judge not, lest you be judged." In today's tolerant spirit and sensitivity over political correctness, the no-nonsense church conveys to her people the truth of Scripture, even though it stands in opposition to the popularized thinking of society. One of the most common beliefs, begging for the clarity of God's Word, concerns the admonition against judging each other. The statement of our Lord condemning false judgments is endlessly quoted out of context and applied to situations that stand in defiance of the Lord's own teachings.

The Scriptures clearly teach that we are to make judgments.[40] God's people are to judge right from wrong. They are to judge sin and evil. Christians are to judge wrongdoing. The church is not to judge only the sin, but the sinner as well.[41] Paul expresses this clearly when he says, "I have written you in my letter not to associate with sexually immoral people – not at all meaning the people of the world who are immoral, or the greedy and swindlers, or idolaters. In that case you would have to leave this world. But now I am writing you that you must not associate with anyone who calls himself a brother but is sexually immoral or greedy, an idolater or a slanderer, a drunkard or a swindler. With such a man do not even eat.

What business is it of mine to judge those outside the church? Are you not to judge those inside? God will judge those outside. 'Expel the wicked man from among you.'"[42]

Endless examples are given in God's Word to understand that God's people are used by God to deliver his judgments. As instruments of truth, we are to faithfully convey the Law of God. In this great servant task as God's spokespersons, we are to, first of all, rightfully judge ourselves.[43] We are to remain humbled by the reality that anytime we have a finger pointing, three more are pointing back at us. We ourselves are poor sinful beings and if we ever lose sight of this Scriptural truth we have failed to make a proper judgment.[44]

Scripture teaches that there are primarily three improper ways by which his people cast judgments against each other.

1. hypocritical, holier-than-thou, judgments,
2. arrogant improper judgments that elevate self as the Law-Giver by calling good evil and evil good and thereby condemning others for not following man made laws,
3. And false judgments that elevate self as God by claiming to know another's motivation or intentions when only God can read the heart and mind of another.

Christ taught, ""Do not judge, or you too will be judged. For in the same way you judge others, you will be judged, and with the measure you use, it will be measured to you."[45] Christ was condemning hypocritical judgments whereby the person sitting in judgment was just as guilty, if not more so, as the person judged. This holier-than-thou attitude in dealing with others was strongly condemned by Christ in the Sermon on the Mount; "Why do you look at the speck of sawdust in your brother's eye and pay no attention to the plank in your own eye? How can you say to your brother, 'Let me take the speck out of your eye, when all the time there is a plank in your own eye? You hypocrite, first take the plank out of your own eye, and then you will see clearly to remove the speck from your brother's eye."[46]

Notice that after a person has dealt with himself in humility and repentance he is then to respond as his brother's keeper. A close companion to the infamously used quote, "judge not, lest you be judged," is the question, "who am I to judge my brother?" Often asked under the disguise of responsible love, avoidance of brotherly admonition is easily revealed by Scripture as false humility. To step aside and allow the passage of a brother's destructive behavior is to fail miserably at loving the brother.

Only God is able to judge one's secret thoughts, but we are to judge man's words and deeds. Only God will bring the world into final judgment when everything is exposed, as the Scriptures testify, "Therefore judge nothing before the appointed time; wait till the Lord comes. He will bring to light what is hidden in darkness and will expose the motives of men's hearts."[47] Only God is able to make judgments of the heart while we are to judge one by the fruit of his/her lips and the deeds of life according to the Word of God. Therefore, Paul instructs us in regards to casting proper judgments that we "do not go beyond what is written."[48]

Jesus followed the condemnation of hypocritical judgments with the words, "Do not give dogs what is sacred; do not throw your pearls to pigs."[49] Jesus commanded, "Stop judging by mere appearances, and make a right judgment."[50] Christians speak like we are not to judge anything that anyone says or does. How absurd to condemn all judgments in light of Scripture's stern warnings to separate ourselves from the evildoer and not mix light with darkness.[51] How are we to understand these directives if we are not to judge aright? Discernment in making appropriate judgments comes from the authority of God's Word alone.

Paul also warns against making improper judgments. He says, "Accept him whose faith is weak, without passing judgment on disputable matters."[52] Paul is speaking against elevating one's self as the Law Giver. "Therefore let us stop passing judgment on one another."[53] The focus, Paul reminds us, ought to be on our brother's need. "Each of us should please his neighbor for his good, to build him up."[54]

James speaks against judging with the same concerns in mind. He admonishes, "Brothers, do not slander one another. Anyone who speaks against his brother or judges him speaks against the law and judges it. When you judge the law, you are not keeping it, but sitting in judgment on it. There is only one Law Giver and

Judge, the One who is able to save and destroy. But you – who are you to judge your neighbor?"[55]

Like Paul, James is forbidding the judging of someone else because of freedom issues, i.e. what one eats, drinks, wears, etc. Condemning someone because his tastes or race or actions are not up to par with what you think they should be is a gross violation of the love of Christ. Improper judgments seek to play the role of God who alone is the Law Giver. Paul admonishes, "Therefore do not let anyone judge you by what you eat or drink, or with regard to a religious festival, a New Moon celebration or a Sabbath day. These are a shadow of the things that were to come, the reality, however, is found in Christ."[56]

The Spirit of God graces us with true humility. In the genuineness of faith we enter into the revelation of God's love. The fruit of the Spirit does not allow the possessor of faith to walk away from a brother caught up in the destructive power of sin. Any attempts to wash our hands of responsible behavior towards one another recalls not only the infamous judge of our Lord, Pontius Pilate, but also the first murder investigation.

Remember the first murder crime scene whereby God played the role of detective in interrogating the prime suspect (who also happened to be the guilty party)? The Lord directs the question to Cain, "Where is your brother Abel?"[57] Cain's infamous reply, "Am I my brother's keeper?" was his attempt at avoiding responsibility and covering up his dastardly deed.[58] Throughout the Old and New Testaments, Scripture answers Cain's question with an unquestionable "yes!" The Spirit empowered church is God's instrument on earth to seek and to save those who are lost. We are our brother's keepers and woe to us if we do not call a spade a spade and warn the brother about his sin.[59]

One can hardly read much of the New Testament without being exposed to the continual call for Christians to turn away from a life of sin. For fear of perverting the Gospel, ministries anchored in the grace of Christ appear to experience the greatest angst in law applications. There is surely a delicate balance to be achieved in correctly handling the word of truth.[60]

Thank God that the church empowered by the Spirit engages the Body in admonishment, confession of sin, repentance and faith.[61] Paul reminds the church to "Let the word of Christ dwell in you richly as you teach and admonish one another with all wisdom."[62] "Put to death, therefore, whatever belongs to your earthly nature."[63] "You must rid yourselves of all such things."[64] Christ ever calls out to His church, "Repent and do the things you did at first. If you do not repent, I will come to you and remove your lamp stand from its place."[65] "He who has an ear, let him hear what the Spirit says to the churches."[66]

Grace is cheapened when the church fails to value the high price by which God's forgiveness was brought to us. Not with gold or silver, but with the precious blood of the Son of God. The Spirit brings conviction of sin and turns the heart of the sinner towards the love of a Savior. With a new heart the believer does not consent to sin, even though he sins, rather he repents in sorrow and rejoices in faith. Paul says, "Therefore, do not let sin reign in your mortal body so that you obey its evil desires."[67] "For sin shall not be your master, because you are not under law, but under grace."[68] The Spirit empowered church brings the message of forgiveness to a weak and poor sinful membership.

When the church gathers for worship, a word of absolution ought to always be spoken. For God has called together his people to hear the message of forgiveness in Christ. The blood of the Lamb of God has atoned for the sins of all who repent and trust in Christ alone for salvation. To withhold the Gospel proclamation, from those for whom God has prepared to receive such good news, is abominable. Conversely, to convey forgiveness apart from a repentant heart or faith in the Savior is a perversion of the truth. We worship in Spirit and Truth.[69]

The glorious Gospel proclaims forgiveness of sin through faith in Christ. The good news is that the atonement for sin has been finalized in the death of our Lord on the cross. The awesome reality conveyed in Christ is that sin, death and the devil are forever defeated. This victory is all the more reason for a no tolerance stance against sin and evil.

The Law of God only terrifies and condemns the hearts of sinners. The Gospel of Christ uplifts the soul and leads to repentant hearts embracing true faith. The law, in the absence of the confessions of sin and faith, leads the heart into despair, while the good news of a forgiving Savior empowers the heart with hope everlasting.

God's Spirit drives out fear, enabling the believer to welcome the Law. The Law becomes the guide by which the Christian is able to discern the will of God. The sinful nature will ever haunt the child of God in this veil of tears. Through the message of Christ, the Spirit continues to work repentance over sin and trust in Christ for forgiveness, life, and salvation.[70] The Gospel is the power of God for the salvation of everyone who believes.[71]

The no-nonsense church is engaged in the celebrations of rejoicing among her members. She is also intensely involved in the mourning of her member's losses. Ministry that exhibits a cold distance to her members' joys and sorrows quenches the Spirit that ever moves us towards a rich intimacy in the bond of Jesus Christ. The fruit of the Holy Spirit are expressive of this bond. Any behavior that works in opposition to the Spirit's fruit hinders the Spirit's work and is counter productive to the fellowship of God's people.

More is needed than merely resisting the sin that would destroy our Christian fellowship. The no-nonsense church is proactive in establishing the setting whereby the fruit of the Spirit is encouraged and enhanced. With proper boundaries in place, small group Bible studies may provide an excellent context in which the Spirit's fruit is freely expressed.

The no-nonsense church guards against becoming apathetic and indifferent or oblivious to the needs arising in the fellowship of believers. Organizations may easily take on a life of their own whereby volunteer and paid workers exist to simply oil the machinery and keep the organization afloat, drifting (often aimlessly) in status quo. The no-nonsense church grasps the necessity of ever challenging her members towards maturation in meeting ministry needs by responding to the generosity of God.

Constantly marching forward in faith, there remains a continual need for the church to be "in the Word and on her knees," in order to recognize God given opportunities to serve his people. The no-nonsense church remains on the alert, sober and vigilant, in her desire to be molded after God's will and enfolded into God's plans.

She wants nothing to do with manipulating God in accordance with the plans of man. When the church attempts to fashion God after her agenda, then the ministry is apt to experience endless obstacles.

The church is not in the business of setting God's agenda for how to accomplish his work. The church is an instrument used by God to accomplish his objectives. When God opens the doors, then he supplies the necessary resources. No man can shut the open door provided by our Lord.[72] Congregations have an extremely difficult time cultivating the patience required by being still and waiting upon the Lord. Like the farmer, a congregation is totally dependent upon the Lord to supply.

Patience is a fruit of the Spirit and is a gift of God.[73] The no-nonsense church is always in training, learning better from the Master how to respond to the needs around her. Only God determines the final outcome. The church follows God's agenda and humbly accepts the methods by which God leads.

Paul declares, "Therefore, there is now no condemnation for those who are in Christ Jesus."[74] This applies only where "the law of the Spirit of life set me free from the law of sin and death" through faith in Christ.[75] Christ condemned sin in sinful man, "in order that the righteous requirements of the law might be fully met in us, who do not live according to the sinful nature, but according to the Spirit."[76]

No-nonsense ministries of our Lord are Spirit empowered so that they may ever remain faithful and receive the crown of life.[77] Repentance and faith are the telltale evidence that the Spirit is accomplishing his work in the no-nonsense church of our Lord Jesus Christ. The Spirit presses the Church forward in faith. Congregations are ever moving forward or declining in the accomplishment of their mission. No-nonsense ministries never stand dormant or content with status quo. The day of salvation is dawning. The church engages in the work of God, while it is day, because the night comes when no one can work.[78] In the Spirit's power, faith and love are ever active and maturing as God's people faithfully proclaim the glorious Gospel. May the good Lord who has begun this good work in his people bring it to completion in the day of our Lord Jesus Christ.[79]

Digging Deeper into the Word of God

1. Read 1 Corinthians 2:6-16. Why is the Spirit absolutely necessary for the understanding of truth? (see 1 Corinthians 12:3) Why is the presence of the Spirit equated with the "mind of Christ"? What statements in this group of verses provide hope and comfort?

2. Read Romans 8:5-17. According to these verses what is the role of the Spirit of God in the life lived by God's people? What is the role of the Holy Spirit in the identity issues of God's people? What does the Spirit of God insure on the part of the children of the Heavenly Father? How are people different who do not possess the Spirit of Christ?

3. Read Revelation 3:1-6. What is the identifiable problem with the Sardis congregation? Jesus calls upon the church to wake up. Has your church ever experienced a wake up call from God? How and when? What does it mean that Christ did not find their deeds complete in God's eyes? If God were to give your church a wake up call today, what do you think would be the identified problem/s?

4. Read Ephesians 4:29-32. How has the Holy Spirit sealed God's people for the day of redemption? In what ways does Paul suggest a Christian might grieve the Spirit of God? What are the characteristics listed that should be rejected by God's people? Do these ungodly behaviors have a strangle hold on people you know? On your congregation? How does your church proactively adorn the characteristics of verse 32?

5. Read 1 Thessalonians 4:1-8. What is the direct connection between the giving of God's Spirit and holy living? What does it mean to be sanctified in verse 3? What is the connection between self-control and knowing God, conveyed in verses 4-5? Verse 8 verifies the role of the Holy Spirit in revealing the will of God for his people. What else does verse 8 assert?

6. Memorize Galatians 5:22-23; "But the fruit of the Spirit is love, joy, peace, patience, kindness, goodness, faithfulness, gentleness and self-control. Against such things there is no law."

Endnotes

[1] Psalm 119:105

[2] Romans 8:9

[3] Titus 3:5b-6

[4] Matthew 28:18-20

[5] Mark 16:16

[6] Matthew 26:26-29; Mark 14:22-25; Luke 22:17-20; John; and St. Paul in 1 Corinthians 11:23-25

[7] 1 Corinthians 11:27-32

[8] John 16:7b-11

[9] John 3:8

[10] 1 Corinthians 12:3

[11] Romans 8:4

[12] 1 Thessalonians 5:19

[13] 1 Thessalonians 5:16-18

[14] 1 Thessalonians 5:20-22

[15] Ephesians 5:18b

[16] Ephesians 5:19-20

[17] 1 Corinthians 12:7

[18] Ephesians 4:12-13

[19] Luke 18:9-14

[20] Newton, John, *Amazing Grace*, Olney Hymns (London: W. Oliver, 1779), public domain.

[21] see Galatians 5:16-26

[22] 1 John 1:8-10

[23] Psalm 1:1-2

[24] see Chapter 10

[25] Ephesians 4:27

[26] Galatians 5:16-17

[27] Galatians 5:22-24

[28] Galatians 5:25-26

[29] Matthew 6:12

[30] Galatians 6:1-2

[31] Matthew 18:15-17

[32] Matthew 18:15

[33] Romans 6:1-2

[34] Malachi 2:16

[35] Ephesians 2:3b

[36] 1 Corinthians 6:9-10

[37] 2 John: 8

[38] Hebrews 12:1

[39] James 1:27

[40] One of endless examples is Matthew 7:15

[41] i.e. 1 Corinthians 5:13

[42] 1 Corinthians 5:9-13

[43] Matthew 7:5

[44] 1 John 1:8

[45] Matthew 7:1-2

[46] Matthew 7:3-5

[47] 1 Corinthians 3:5

[48] 1 Corinthians 3:6

[49] Matthew 7:6

[50] John 7:24 (cf. Galatians 2:6 whereby Paul reminds us that God does not judge by outward experiences)

[51] 2 Corinthians 6:14, 17

[52] Romans 14:1

[53] Romans 14:13

[54] Romans 15:2

[55] James 4:11-12

[56] Colossians 2:16-17

[57] Genesis 4:9

[58] Genesis 4:9

[59] Ezckiel 3:18-21

[60] 2 Timothy 2:15

[61] Galatians 6:1

[62] Colossians 3:16

[63] Colossians 3:5

[64] Colossians 3:8 (cf. 1 Peter 2:1-3; 1 Thessalonians 4:1-8)

[65] Revelation 2:5b-6

[66] Revelation 2:7
[67] Romans 6:12
[68] Romans 6:14
[69] John 4:24
[70] Romans 10:17
[71] Romans 1:16
[72] Revelation 3:7; 2 Corinthians 2:12
[73] Galatians 5:22
[74] Romans 8:1
[75] Romans 8:2
[76] Romans 8:3-4
[77] Revelation 2:10
[78] John 9:4
[79] Philippians 1:6

Chapter 4 – Faith Driven
(or "When Did Comfortable Become the End Game?")

*"But we are not of those who shrink back and are destroyed,
but of those who believe and are saved."*
Hebrews 10:39

Our daughter, Jennifer, returned from a two-week mission trip to Cherepovets, Russia and, as usual, felt that she received more than was able to give. Since few missionaries come to America on mission trips, God sends Americans overseas to learn the meaning of faith. On her trip to Russia, Jennifer would not be disappointed in her desire for a deeper faith.

The work in Russia centered on the operation of a Christian camp, a very primitive tent camp. Jennifer recalls one day when it was raining that the Americans all ran for shelter and were incessantly complaining, groaning and moaning about how their activities had been upset. The Russian Christians stayed out in the rain for a while longer and then meandered into the shelter. Instead of complaining about the weather they broke out in song, singing, "How Great Thou Art!" in Russian. Humbled by the experience, the Americans followed by singing the same in English. Jennifer noted how the entire atmosphere changed and everyone began laughing and making the best of the situation. Faith believes God remains on the job in every circumstance.

A person knows whether a church operates according to faith by her adopted priorities. Because no-nonsense ministries are centered in Christ and empowered by the Spirit of God they are faith driven. Faith grabs a firm hold on the moment, any moment, and trusts in God for whatever is needed. Faith depends upon God for meaning and purpose in the present circumstances. Faith firmly believes that "in all things God works for the good of those who love him, who have been called according to his purpose."[1]

Faith based ministries operate around a supernatural ability to trust in God alone. Faith looks to God for all things. Faith wraps its arms around God's promised presence and hangs on for dear life. Faith looks up to God in all situations. Faith denies the accidental nature of life and rejects the concepts of luck. Anchored in the confidence of God's love, faith rises to meet every day afresh in the expectation of God's plan.

Faith equals trust. Faith is not only a grasp of the truth, but a trust in the truth. Faith is not just a virtue we cling to; faith is a value we live. So often faith is reduced to an intellectual understanding of revelation. Doctrinal acuity is valuable only if accompanied by the heart. Scripture reminds us that the demons have intellectual faith and shudder.[2]

Faith is supernatural. Faith is God's work. Faith is a gift of God created by the power of his Holy Spirit.[3] No one can make a true confession of faith unless the Holy Spirit has worked such faith in the heart.[4] In the no-nonsense church, faith draws Christians together for worship and service in Christ. Faith is not treated as a side issue in the Christian life. Faith in Christ is THE issue insuring the blessings of life and salvation.

Paul instructs God's people to work out their salvation with fear and trembling.[5] This is not possible without the gift of faith. "For it is God who works in you to will and to act according to his good purpose."[6] Faith is the key that unlocks the door of life, Jesus Christ.[7] Christ brings life abundant.[8] No other door provides the way and no other key opens the door.

The no-nonsense church remains astutely aware of the need to exercise faith in all things. God spoke through the prophet Habakkuk, "the righteous will live by his faith."[9] The writer to the Hebrews encourages God's people to not give up on faith. He says, "So do not throw away your confidence; it will be richly rewarded. You need to persevere so that when you have done the will of God, you will receive what he has promised. For in just a very little while, 'He who is coming will come and will not delay. But my righteous one will live by faith. And if he shrinks back, I will not be pleased with him. But we are not of those who shrink back and are destroyed, but of those who believe and are saved."[10]

Churches may give rhetoric to faith while simultaneously laying aside the principles of faith. Churches proceed to operate around a humanistic and corporate world mindset. The temptation to replace godly faith with secular business principles is huge. The church operates in the world where financial wealth reigns. Too often ministries are seduced into dependence upon the almighty dollar instead of the Almighty Savior. Faith ever remains on guard against the enslavement to the things of this world.

The no-nonsense church deeply resists the temptations to become dependent upon anything other than God. Her confidence remains upon what God has said, what God has done, what God has worked, what God has supplied, what God has promised and what God seeks to accomplish through the Body of Jesus Christ. No-nonsense ministries do not just talk about this dependency they are dependent. The no-nonsense church does not just talk the talk of faith, she walks the walk of faith. In attitude and behavior, in word and deed, God's people live according to their faith. Through the study of Scripture, in repentance and abiding trust, in humble prayer and all decision-making, the no-nonsense church is constantly called into the accountability of dependence upon God by exercising the gift of faith.

Faith driven ministries keep their eyes on Jesus through thick or thin. They do not allow circumstances or needs to distract them from the "main thing." The no-nonsense church knows all too well that the testing of faith develops the ability to persevere. The ability to hang in with faith during difficult times is necessary so that God's people may reach their best in Christ.[11] Peter informs us that the fruit of faith is absolutely essential for God's people to remain effective and productive. In the absence of a maturing and growing faith, the church becomes nearsighted and blind.[12]

Paul instructs Timothy in the way of the faith, so that by remaining faithful his spiritual son "may fight the good fight, holding on to the faith and a good conscience."[13] Conversely, Paul notes, "Some have shipwrecked their faith."[14] This holds true for congregations as much as it holds true for individual Christians. When the day is done, the no-nonsense church strives to declare with Paul, "I have fought the good fight, I have finished the race, I have kept the faith."[15]

No-nonsense ministries that are driven by faith are not easily sidetracked in attaining to their purpose. Faith driven ministries invoke God's people towards total dependency upon God. Such dependency involves a three-fold emphasis that encourages God's people to be in the Word, on their knees, and looking beyond themselves. Continually engaged with divine and human relationship activities, the no-nonsense church strives to develop the culture of dependency. This flies in the face of today's individualism.

When a church is challenged by a lack of resources, faith driven ministries fall to their knees with the cry of their hearts grounded in what God has promised. No-nonsense ministries do not have their hands tightly grasped around their self-made agendas, refusing to let go of their plans at all costs. Faith driven ministries have their hands tightly grasped around the Word of God and refuse to let go of God's plans and promises revealed.

When the ministry's plans encounter a closed door, the no-nonsense church does not immediately abandon ship or, conversely, blast through the door anyway. In response to identifiable but unreachable opportunities of ministry, faith driven ministries reposition themselves to dig deeper into the counsel of God and wait for the Spirit's guidance. The no-nonsense church clings to God's promise through James, "If any of you lacks wisdom, he should ask God, who gives generously to all without finding fault, and it will be given to him. But when he asks, he must believe and not doubt, because he who doubts is like a wave of the sea, blown and tossed by the wind. That man should not think he will receive anything from the Lord; he is a double-minded man, unstable in all he does."[16]

No church's journey comes complete with a detailed map and a set of plans outlining the specific steps along the way. Just as children are born to parents who have never journeyed into parenthood, so God gives birth to ministries that have no prior experience in walking with God. But, unlike first time parents who are not given a manual on how to raise their child, the church possesses a manual in which is revealed all she needs to operate.

This reality becomes a primary instigator in promoting a church's dependency upon the Word of God. God does not expect a church to know what he has not revealed. God does expect a church to cling tightly to the revelation given, while trusting in him to move the ministry along the path he has planned for her to travel. The Word of God may not answer every question raised nor provide the specifics in utilizing the God-given resources provided, but the church has all the directives she needs to operate under the blessings and grace of God. As she adheres to what God has instructed, God's providence and sovereignty will direct the outcome needed.

As typical, this is all easier said than accomplished. The flesh is apt to interfere. Ministries may take on a life of their own and become extremely thick headed and stubborn in the desire to hang on to self made agendas. Redeemed, but still sinful, people of God may develop creative justifications and rationalizations for laying aside faith in God and doing their own thing in God's name. The crowd persuasively follows the boisterous leader who refuses to consider alternative solutions to the obstacles encountered. An outspoken member may forcefully intimidate the majority into blindness of the real needs of a congregation. Blinded by their own opinions, leaders often oppose the opportunities that exist to effectively share the Gospel of Christ. Wise old Solomon said, "Wisdom is better than weapons of war, but one sinner destroys much good."[17] This engages the ministry in much nonsense!

The setting of the ministry's budget can also be a challenging exercise of faith. Discerning the boundaries between realistic faith and foolish faith is needed. Sometimes the boundaries are obvious, but frequently they are not clearly discerned. Wisdom from above is sincerely sought by being "in the Word and on the knees."

Everyone one has his or her pet project or specific interest. This is to be expected, considering the wide range of gifts that our gracious God has distributed amidst his people. However, every ministry operates around limitations in this world. To attempt a few mission endeavors well is preferred over adopting a wide range of commitments done poorly. A church can easily stretch her resources too far. Wisdom, guided and determined by faith, is needed. Wisdom is the practical application of the knowledge of God.

Faith understands that with God all things are possible.[18] Faith responds with Paul, "I can do everything through him who gives me strength."[19] Faith anticipates the necessary gifts to appropriately respond to the calling of God. Faith looks for the doors that God has opened. Faith also accepts the reality of the miraculous and expects great gifts from a great God. Faith seeks God's guidance in the mystery of God's work. Faith looks for God to provide direction every step of the way.

This faith relationship, originating in God's love, entangles us in the exercise of faithful prayer. Faith driven ministries adhere to the teachings of Christ concerning asking, seeking, and knocking. Jesus promised to his followers, "Ask and it will be given to you; seek and you will find; knock and the door will be opened to you. For everyone who asks receives; he who seeks finds; and to him who knocks, the door will be opened. Which of you, if his son asks for bread, will give him a stone? Or if he asks for a fish, will give him a snake? If you, then, though you are evil, know how to give good gifts to your children, how much more will your Father in heaven give good gifts to those who ask him!"[20]

Asking, seeking and knocking are not disconnected to each other whereby a person may choose one over the other. Nor are they synonymous terms. Petitioning God simultaneously creates the need to listen attentively, whereby the petitioner seeks a Word from God. Seeking, in the context of prayer, communicates that we are truly seeking God's Word, his guidance, will and blessings, not the fulfillment of our own preconceived, predetermined desires. Both activities, laying our needs and wants on the table of God's presence and humbly sitting at his feet to listen, engages us in knocking, whereby we commit ourselves to travel through the door of life. This door of life is none other than the way of Christ, for the door is Christ himself conveyed in the Gospel.[21]

Faith clings to the promises of receiving and finding. Faith trusts in the promise of open doors. Faith driven ministries develop the humility of boldness that possesses confidence in the promises of God. The shamelessness in which God's people approach the Heavenly Father for their needs rests entirely on the forgiving message through faith in Christ. The Gospel alone empowers the no-nonsense church in her confident asking, seeking, and knocking. The boldness of humility in approaching God entirely rests in the blood of the Lamb sacrificed on the cross for our sins. Only in our forgiven state through faith in Christ are we invited, much less able, to approach God as a friend requested to meet our needs.

The ministry is, in one sense, an expression of the collective trust of God's people in the Gospel of Jesus Christ. Every ministry involvement and every ministry relationship is expressive and mindful of this trust. Faith produces faith activities. If the integrity of faith is excluded from a particular endeavor that engages the ministry's efforts, then it is most assuredly part of the nonsense camp. This may be the case because a particular activity never was an appropriate aspect of the ministry or it may be because the endeavor has changed hats. Regardless of the reason, when the limited resources of ministry are directed towards efforts that are separated from the ingredients of faith in Jesus Christ, then at best the trivial devours the meaningful.

Not only are faith driven ministries dependent upon God, but they also operate in recognition of their need for each other. The no-nonsense church understands clearly that she is not called to be an island unto herself; any more than individual Christians can live God-pleasing lives separated from the Body. Every local group of Christians gathered for kingdom work retains a keen interest in the accomplishments and struggles of other congregations in which they share a common faith around the world.

The interdependence that God designs, especially between members of the localized congregations, creates the need for gift recognition. Acknowledgement of the resources that God has supplied the Body, through his people, to accomplish the work of ministry is pertinent to utilizing such resources for the common good.[22] The expectation that God's people will supply the ministry with the necessary gifts naturally follows the confidence that God's people are in possession of those gifts. The no-nonsense church exercises faith in God's promises to supply his Body with all that she needs.[23]

While faith is the most acknowledged virtue in the Christian Church it is not the most utilized with regards to practical operations. Ministries often speak with forked tongue when decisions are made concerning the mission of the church. Calling upon faith, the church then succumbs to decisions that speak only human logic. The issue is not that decisions should defy logic, but simply that they should not defy faith either. To limit the scope of ministry to only that which can be clearly seen, anticipated and understood is to disregard the faith that is necessary to journey with God.

Faith leads us down paths we would not otherwise travel. The path of faith is a road less traveled primarily because of the disappointments, hardships, trials and sufferings encountered. In the flesh, humans avoid such journeys. Christians welcome the path of greatest resistance whenever the Spirit is prompting the voyage. The no-nonsense church endures all hardship, as discipline from God.[24] She knows all too well that "If you do not stand firm in your faith, you will not stand at all."[25] Faith driven ministries remember the days gone by when they stood their ground in the face of suffering precisely because they had faith in God's deliverance. The no-nonsense church does not throw away her confidence. She knows that such faith will be richly rewarded. "You need to persevere so that when you have done the will of God, you will receive what he has promised."[26]

Faith never calls upon the church to lay aside doing what is right for expedient reasons. Nor does faith ever willingly violate the expressed will of God. Faith always does what is right according to the revealed Word of God. If the church concludes that she must ignore the will of God in order to accomplish her mission or provide adequate resources for ministry, then she has surely over-stepped her bounds. Such over-extension on the part of a congregation is equivalent to adopting man's agenda over and against God's plans.

A common violation of this reality may be observed in the inadequate compensations of church workers. When the church cannot compensate her workers appropriately then she is living beyond her God-given means. Nonsense exists wherever those who serve the church are expected to bear the burden of the membership's poor stewardship practices and the church's overextension decisions.

God pleasing stewardship not only concerns itself with how much money is spent, but how the money spent is utilized to support the ministry of Jesus Christ. [27]

The no-nonsense church is driven by her faith to do the will of God. Maybe in some sense it's just a semantic difference, but the church is driven, not by her mission or her purpose, but by her confidence in God. Contrary to what has been emphasized since the birth of the "church growth movement," the church does not exist to multiply but to faithfully proclaim Christ. Her faith is what keeps her focused on the mission to share Christ. In this way God multiplies the number of those who believe.

The no-nonsense church is driven to share her faith in Christ precisely because she possesses it. Believers are determined to let their light shine because the light shines in their hearts. We are resolute to give testimony to what God has done for others because of what He has specifically done for us. The task of the church is not to save the world, but to proclaim to the world her Savior. Only Jesus Christ is the world's Savior. The church is driven by faith in Christ to let the Gospel be known among the nations. The no-nonsense church is mission focused.[28]

My first cousin who belonged to the church where I was a pastor use to inquire from me on a weekly basis, "What is the sermon about this Sunday?" To which I would always reply the same, "Faith!" Faith is what drives me to preach. Faith is what calls me to be a pastor. Sermons may express variant themes covering a host of Biblical topics, but central to every Christian message is faith in Christ.

Faith continues to express the ability of the church to trust in God for all that she is, has been, and hopes to be. She is the Body of Christ and in Christ she places her faith. The no-nonsense church resists the temptation to manipulate, devise or scheme so that "man's" ministry plans may come to fruition. Rather than praying that God blesses the church's plans, no-nonsense ministries fall on their knees in continual prayer asking God to use them in his plans.

Discernment is needed. The Spirit provides what is needed through the revelation of God. The church does best to dig deeper into the living Word. Could it be that God seeks his people to redirect, rearrange or cleanse their plans after his will? Maybe that is why doors remain shut. Faith waits for the wisdom that descends from above. There is often a fine line between manipulating the ministry after our own will and wrestling with the fulfillment of God's will. The flesh always seeks to intrude upon the spirit in these matters.[29]

As God's people respond with the fruit of faith, he will supply the wisdom needed to move forward in faith.[30] The no-nonsense church, in response to closed doors or inadequate resources, burrows herself in the Word of God and remains in constant prayer. Maybe this is the very thing that the Lord prompts prior to opening the floodgate of blessings. Or, maybe God desires to redirect the church's focus towards another door of opportunity, bringing to the attention some need being overlooked. Maybe God wants us to bury our predetermined agendas and let his plan arise. Regardless, where faith is digging, the Spirit is working.

The soul of Israel was in danger of becoming lost in the safety of enslavement. Faith is freedom. Faith brings freedom from all that would enslave the flesh. Faith overcomes the flesh. Faith overcomes fear. Faith drives Abraham up on the mountain of God to give it all up – all confidence in the flesh, in human dreams and shortsighted hopes. Faith is a risky, dangerous business, an adventure, and the call of the Spirit. Faith takes you to places unknown where fear threatens your very identity. The journey of faith takes you through the wilderness into God's promised land. There is no other way to get there.

The Spirit drives Israel into the wilderness. So also Abraham, Jacob, Elijah, John the Baptist, Paul and all others who let God remain in the driver's seat of life. The Spirit drove the very incarnate Son of God into the wilderness of Satan's temptations. In the wilderness you have to dispel the darkness. Flesh screams to go back to the safety and comfort of the familiar. Faith says go forward; there is no turning back. Faith tames the flesh while releasing the Spirit's passionate love gone wild. Fear settles the soul in mediocrity while in the Spirit the soul soars the mountain peaks of eagles.

The no-nonsense church lives by faith, not by sight.[31] She is confident of God's presence because she trusts in God's promises. And she lives in the light of hope eternal. For she has been "crucified with Christ" and the life she lives is the life of Christ within. As

Paul says, "The life I live in the body, I live by faith in the Son of God, who loved me and gave himself for me."[32] The Body of Christ longs to journey home where her Savior is seen face to face. The Church aches to know, as she has been known.[33] She anticipates the joy of the kingdom everlasting. In good times and bad, in smooth or rough sailing through the waters of life, the no-nonsense church prays, "Come, Lord Jesus, come!"[34]

Faith that expels the fear of darkness is willing to die, rather than turn back towards the fake and phony, the superficial or trivial. To be driven refers to the energizing force of an action. Faith, empowered by the Spirit, grounded in the Word of God, and centered in Christ is beyond question the driving force in the life of the no-nonsense church. "So those who have faith are blessed along with Abraham, the man of faith."[35]

Discernment will always be needed between faith and foolishness to guard against man's attempts at passing off his agendas as God ordained. But no-nonsense ministries know that trusting in God for all that is needed is never foolish. In fact, the no-nonsense church trusts, first of all, that God will justly determine what is really needed. In God alone the Church finds refuge. The no-nonsense church proclaims "without faith it is impossible to please God."[36]

Paul's words to Timothy are suitably applied to every individual member belonging to the Church of Jesus Christ: "Some people, eager for money, have wandered from the faith and pierced themselves with many griefs. But you, man of God, flee from all this, and pursue righteousness, godliness, faith, love, endurance and gentleness. Fight the good fight of the faith. Take hold of the eternal life to which you were called when you made your good confession in the presence of many witnesses. In the sight of God, who gives life to everything, and of Christ Jesus, who while testifying before Pontius Pilate made the good confession, I charge you to keep this command without spot or blame until the appearing of our Lord Jesus Christ, which God will bring about in his own time – God, the blessed and only Ruler, the King of kings and Lord of lords, who alone is immortal and who lives in unapproachable light, whom no one has seen or can see. To him be honor and might forever. Amen."[37]

Digging Deeper into the Word of God

1. Read Ephesians 2:8-10. What does this passage say about faith? If faith itself is a gift of God what does that say about our dependency upon God for ministry? How is faith more than mere intellectual assent? According to verse 10, how is faith connected to God's plan that we engage in good works?

2. Read Hebrews 11. This is considered the great faith chapter of the Bible. People of true faith live as strangers in this world (verse 13). What does it mean to live as foreigners on earth? People of true faith have their eyes set on the hope to come in Christ. Why is God not ashamed of them according to verse 16? Faith calls God's people together. How is receiving what God has promised connected to believers of the past (verse 40)?

3. Read Romans 12:2-3. How are God's people to offer their bodies as living sacrifices? What are examples of people who conform to the patterns of this world? How might your congregation resist the temptation to reflect the world instead of Christ? What does Paul mean that Christians are to be transformed? How do churches test and approve the will of God? How does the knowledge that God has worked faith in his people in varying measures assist them in working together as a church? How does arrogance work against faith?

4. Read James 2:14-26. According to James, what is the connection between faith and works? Is it possible for faith to be void of all works? What is a good work in the eyes of God? Read Hebrews 11:6. What does this say about works void of faith? Read 1 Corinthians 13:1-3. What does this say about works or faith void of love? Read John 15:5. What does this say about producing fruit? Read Romans 3:28. Do good works contribute to one's salvation?

5. Read Galatians 3:23-25. In what ways were people held prisoner by the law? How does the law lead us to Christ? What does it mean

to be justified? If believers are no longer under the supervision of the law, then why do they strive to obey it? Read Romans 3:31.

6. Memorize Galatians 2:20; "I have been crucified with Christ and I no longer live, but Christ lives in me. The life I live in the body, I live by faith in the Son of God, who loved me and gave himself for me."

Endnotes

[1] Romans 8:28

[2] James 2:19

[3] Ephesian 2:8-9

[4] 1 Corinthians 12:3

[5] Philippians 2:12

[6] Philippians 2:13

[7] John 3:16; 20:31

[8] John 10:10

[9] Habakkuk 2:4; quoted by St. Paul in Romans 1:7 and Galatians 3:11

[10] Hebrews 10:35-39

[11] James 1:2-3

[12] 2 Peter 1:5-9

[13] 1 Timothy 1:18

[14] 1 Timothy 1:19; 6:12

[15] 2 Timothy 4:7

[16] James 1:5-8

[17] Ecclesiastes 9:18

[18] Matthew 19:26

[19] Philippians 4:13

[20] Matthew 7:7-12

[21] John 14:6

[22] 1 Corinthians 12:7

[23] Matthew 6:33

[24] Hebrews 12:7

[25] Isaiah 7:9

[26] Hebrews 10:31b-36

[27] see chapter 7: "Mission Focused"

[28] 1 Timothy 5:17-18 (cf. chapter 8; "Generosity Exemplified")

[29] Romans 8:14-25

[30] Hebrews 13:15-16

[31] 2 Corinthians 5:7

[32] Galatians 2:20

[33] 1 Corinthians 13:12

[34] Revelation 22:20

[35] Galatians 3:9

[36] Hebrews 11:6

[37] 1 Timothy 6:10b-16

Chapter 5 – Love Motivated
(or "What's Love Got To Do With It?")

*"For Christ's love compels us, because we are convinced
that one died for all, and therefore all died."*
2 Corinthians 5:14

My wife's great grandfather, a German immigrant to this country in 1843, passed down through his ancestry the following story:

An Indian lost in the woods came to the door of a white settler one night asking for something to eat. The white man said he could not give him food and told him to move on. The Indian had to wait until morning to find his way home. Later, it happened that the same white settler lost his way and upon getting dark he met an Indian and asked him the way back to the white settlement. He recognized the Indian whom he had turned away one night.

The Indian told him to follow him. He took him to the Indian settlement, gave him food and provided him shelter. It was the Indian way of showing esteem to visitors. The white man did not sleep all night thinking that the Indian would take revenge on him, but since the Indian did not show any signs of knowing him he had hopes he would not be identified.

The next morning they got up and he was offered breakfast. The Indian told him to follow again. So he did. He was lead to a trail and the Indian told him to follow the trail that would lead to the settlement of the whites. But, before he departed, he asked the white man, "Do you remember when a redskin was at the door of a white man on a cold winter night and the white man refused to give food or shelter?" He had to admit he did. Then the Indian added, "Redskin different man, gives white man food and shelter on dark night."[1]

Those in whom the living Spirit of Christ dwells are different people too. They give out of what they have freely received to all who are willing recipients. They pray for the opportunity to love and when the door is opened they rush through it like there is no tomorrow. The joy of the Lord is their strength in loving.[2]

The obligatory nature guiding the response to the opportunities afforded by love has clouded the hearts of many Christians. Gone are the days whereby the majority of those lifting high the cross of Christ do so at great sacrifice and risk to their own welfare. That is my observation in the land of the free and the home of the brave. Self-interest entices away the followers of Christ to become lovers of the world. Those willing to invest time or money to serve others often appear to be motivated only by a sense of duty.

Where are the volunteer soldiers in the Lord's army who are willing to die for their King? I have a pastor friend who when asked, "How are you doing?" always responds, "Blessed by the Lord." How refreshing to remember we live under God's favor because of His great love for us. Most Christians seem to fall into the seductive trap that obsesses over things and promotes the self instead of Christ. The view that one is obligated instead of privileged to respond to God's love is created from heartless souls lacking passionate love for their Savior. Those who dwell in the hope of Christ are truly different people. How shameful when it is otherwise.

No-nonsense ministries are love motivated. Love can be a truly flaky commodity. Love can be reduced to a mere feeling, an emotional high, or a perverted expression of the flesh. Love can be expressed towards things, ideas or relationships. Love remains one of the most inconsistent concepts conveyed. The Bible says, "God is love."[3] Need we say more? Yes, one more thing! "This is love: not that we loved God, but that he loved us and sent his Son as an atoning sacrifice for our sins."[4] Everything God is incorporates his unconditional sacrificial love. The nature of God's presence within his people is love. "Dear friends, since God so loved us, we also ought to love one another. No one has ever seen God; but if we love one another, God lives in us and his love is made complete in us."[5]

The Body of Christ is created, uplifted, motivated, and empowered by the love of God, demonstrated in the death of Christ. Those in whom God lives, inevitably, of necessity, demonstrate love. Apart from the expression of God's love there exists no real value in ministry.[6] The necessity of divine love cannot be overplayed nor overstressed. The church's love, unlike worldly love, originates in her Creator/Redeemer.[7] Motivated by the same love that sent the only begotten Son of God to the cross to pay for the sin of the world, those who confess Jesus Christ as the Savior are compelled to express God's love in all that they seek to accomplish.[8]

When did the love feast in the weekly gatherings of the early church become just a feast? Today people want to feast upon the provisions and blessings of the church as though they have a right to them, without any of love's responsibilities or obligations. "Damn" the church if she is not there to welcome me with open arms and meet my needs. "Damn" the church if she asks from me anything in return. What happened to the compelling love that brought God's people together in order to love each other as they had been loved?

To confess belief in God, who by definition is love, and simultaneously deny the responsibilities of his love towards others is totally nonsense. Those who love God strive to live in his love. Those who refuse to express love towards others deny the love of him whose name they represent.[9] They are worst then unbelievers who outright reject God's love.[10] No-nonsense Christians do not hide God's love. Retaining love for selfish purposes ceases to be God's love and has become a perverted love, originating in the sinful flesh.

The no-nonsense church operates around the demonstration of God's love.[11] All mission statements and strategic ministry plans are varied expressions of sharing the love of a living Christ to a dying world. God's love impacts all that we are and all that we hope to accomplish. No-nonsense ministry is on a quest of love.[12] The question embedded in all questions is "How can we effectively communicate the demonstrative love of God to others?" The Gospel is nothing less than the good news of God's love, demonstrated in the death of Christ and verified by his life.

I get a sense that the majority of churches are too distracted by the trivial and the financial to participate in the radical nature of God's unconditional and sacrificial love. Congregations offer far too many excuses for not seeking out the lost, the lonely, the impoverished, the sick and the dying. If the church happens to stumble across the destitute of society, then maybe (but often not) genuine expressions of love will be given. What a sham for the church as a creation of God's love.

Most churches excel in the rhetoric of love, while lacking in the zeal of love. Where is the congregation that is passionate about the demonstration of love? The lifeblood of the church is derived from the innocent blood of Christ shed on the cross while we were yet sinners.[13] Where is the passion that the recipients of such love demonstrate for each other, much less for the enemies of the faith? Did not Christ say, "Love your enemies and pray for those who persecute you, that you may be sons of your Father in heaven."[14]

Where is the love? Not the misguided love of the world, but the love of God; living, transforming, and impacting the lives of those in contact with the church. We love because He first loved us. "This is how we know what love is: Jesus Christ laid down his life for us. And we ought to lay down our lives for our brothers."[15] Jesus said, "Greater love has no one than this, that he lay down his life for His friends."[16] The no-nonsense church is willing to die, to lay it all on the line, that others might live. We do not need more love rhetoric. The church needs more lovers. John states, "If anyone has material possessions and sees his brother in need but has no pity on him, how can the love of God be in him? Dear children, let us not love with words or tongue but with actions and in truth."[17]

James also reminds us that true faith always expresses itself in good deeds. These works of faith are acts of God's love through us. James says, "Suppose a brother or sister is without clothes and daily food. If one of you says to him, 'Go, I wish you well; keep warm and well fed, but does nothing about his physical needs, what good is it?'"[18] Does this not apply to the collective gathering of God's people, as much as to the individual Christian? Maybe even more so!

In the end, Jesus declares, the sheep are separated from the goats. The sheep are identified as those who displayed a genuine relationship with Christ through faith. "For I was hungry and you gave me something to eat, I was thirsty and you gave me something to drink, I was a stranger and you invited me in, I needed clothes and you clothed me, I was sick and you looked after me, I was in prison and you came to visit me."[19] "I tell you the truth, whatever you did for one of the least of these brothers of mine, you did for me."[20]

The church cannot afford a tolerant spirit towards hate, bitterness, jealousy, gossip, slander, and the like. Any anti-love behavior destroys the works of faith expressing itself through love.[21] God repeatedly warns us against unloving actions. Paul instructs the young pastor Titus to instruct God's people "to slander no one, to be peaceable and considerate, and to show true humility toward all men."[22] Peter instructs, "live in harmony with one another; be sympathetic, love as brothers, be compassionate and humble. Do not repay evil with evil or insult with insult, but with blessing, because to this you were called so that you may inherit a blessing."[23]

John emphatically states, "If anyone says, 'I love God,' yet hates his brother, he is a liar."[24] "Whoever loves God must also love his brother."[25] Violations of love defy the very purpose of the church's existence. If the light of Christ's love is to shine in the darkness it must retain its brightness. Too many churches attempt to carry a torch into the world that has already been extinguished by hate and selfishness. How foolish it must look to a dying world for Christians to parade around a candle whose light has blown out. A loveless church may be well attended, but ineffective.

Apart from God's love the ministry loses her value and worth. God commands the fellowship of believers, "Do not let any unwholesome talk come out of your mouths, but only what is helpful for building others up according to their needs, that it may benefit those who listen. And do not grieve the Holy Spirit of God, with whom you were sealed for the day of redemption. Get rid of all bitterness, rage and anger, brawling and slander, along with every form of malice. Be kind and compassionate to one another, forgiving each other, just as in Christ God forgave you. Be imitators of God, therefore, as dearly loved children and live a life of love, just as Christ loved us and gave himself up for us as a fragrant offering and sacrifice to God."[26]

The no-nonsense church analyzes every communication and action in the light of God's love. Before we can work together we must strive to love together. Peter says, "Above all, love each other deeply."[27] What a defiance of the Spirit of Jesus Christ when Christians come together refusing the bond of God's love. What a fiasco when we slander one another while we work together to love others. No wonder so many churches experience a depth of ineptness. Where the love of God is absent, the power of God is also missing because the Spirit's fire is being extinguished.

The love of God is a demonstration of his power in motion. As Christ moves in and through his people the experience is one of supernatural love. Such love is known by its sacrificial, selfless, and unconditional qualities. "Offer hospitality to one another without grumbling."[28] Beyond man's natural ability to create or sustain, God's love expressed, in Christ, is evidence of God's presence.

The no-nonsense church of our Lord Jesus Christ is love motivated. This truth conveys that Christian love is known and experienced only as God reveals himself to the recipient. Love is a gift of God's presence. Love is a fruit of the indwelling Spirit.[29] Love does not originate within man. Love is engendered in the recipient of divine love. Only in Christ is the supernatural love of God born in the heart. Any expression of love not originating in the truth of God is only temporal and short-lived. Worldly love lacks the ability to sustain itself over time and eternity.

The truth of God is conveyed in the activity of love. The colloquialism "love isn't love until you give it away" expresses this reality. Love in essence is active. God defines love for us by demonstrating love upon the cross. God reveals the true nature of his love by his gift of life. The no-nonsense church views God's sacrificial and unconditional love as the core and essence of true love. God defines love by the activity of his love for us. Paul, in the great love chapter of Scripture, describes love with action words. The reality is that love never remains passive or static. Love is always on the move, always expressing itself, always revealing its true nature. The essence of love lies in its giving nature, originating in the divine gift of life itself.

God says that all of our proclamations and claims to faith, all of our generous gifts and accomplishments, any knowledge of the truth, void of God's love is worthless and of no value.[30] No-nonsense ministries operate around love as defined by God. In order to grasp this great revelation, the church would do well to personalize the definition of love given through Paul.[31] Is our congregation patient and kind? Are we envious, boastful, or proud? Is our congregation rude, selfish, or easily set-off in anger? Do we as members of the Body of Christ remember meticulously the wrongs of others? Does our congregation delight in evil more then we celebrate the truth? Are we in the business of protecting, trusting, hoping, and persevering in the love and truth of Christ?

Christians ought to evaluate in genuine honesty how well love is realized in the fellowship of believers to which they belong. A sinful church needs God's love. A redeemed church not only needs God's love, but she has received it in Christ. God's love transforms the darkness into the light. God's love changes hearts and lives. No-nonsense ministries comprehend divine love as the great enabler of all good things. Love enables patience with one another as the saying expresses, "be patient because God is not through with me." We are an ongoing work of art, fashioned and designed by God's grace, molded into His image and formed by his love. The no-nonsense church acts kindly towards each other as she encourages one another towards love and good deeds until the Day of our Lord Jesus Christ.[32]

Why, then, are so many churches across our land noted for their coldness and uncharitable attitude towards each other, especially the stranger in their midst? This is anti-Christian nonsense? A common evaluation critiquing individual congregations concerns their level of friendliness. "That is not a very friendly church," or "that church is really friendly." All no-nonsense ministries are characterized by the love of Christ and therefore strive to be experienced by others as open, friendly, caring and kind. There are no exceptions to this truth. Violations of this truth occur only when the people of God have ceased to operate in the Spirit and are displaying the characteristics of the flesh.

As a result, confession and repentance are the order of the day, every day. God's people habitually confess their sins to one another in the forgiving love of Christ. Christians engage in acts of kindness towards each other as a fruit of their own humility. They do not envy what God is doing in another's life. They rejoice in the blessings that God is pouring out upon others, for that is an answer to their very prayers. Members of no-nonsense ministries also weep with each other for they are bonded in the love of a Savior who suffered on their behalf.[33]

When God blesses his church, she guards against pride. God's people know that they have not deserved such blessings. Though God may lift them up as examples of his grace and enable them to be leaders among others, children of the Heavenly Father remain humbled by God's amazing love outpoured. Humility prevents the church from becoming rude and self-seeking.

The no-nonsense church is compelled to share God's generous love and let his light be seen. Daily repenting of their own sinful violations of God's love, Christians are not easily angered nor mindful of the sins of others because jealousy, bitterness, hatred, discord, fits of rage, selfish ambition, dissensions, and factions have been replaced by the fruit of the Spirit; "love, joy, peace, patience, kindness, goodness, faithfulness, gentleness and self-control."[34] "Love covers a multitude of sins."[35]

The hearts of God's people are constantly changing. Motivated by God's love and renewed in the Spirit, the Body of Christ prays for open doors to express God's love. All of ministry's endeavors and activities are aimed at sharing the love of Christ with others. This is the truest expression of returning God's love. Jesus proclaimed that our recreated identities as his disciples are revealed in the love that we show one another.[36]

The church motivated by the love of Christ has broken the grip of secular love. The love of things or the love of this world no longer compels the decisions in which Christians engage.[37] God's people are but strangers here; heaven is their home. As aliens in this foreign land (foreign to the nature of God's love) the followers of Christ strive to live in harmony with their Redeemer as a testimony to his redeeming love.

John says, "We know that we have come to know him if we obey his commands. The man who says, 'I know him, but does not do what he commands is a liar, and the truth is not in him. But if anyone obeys his word, God's love is truly made complete in him. This is how we know we are in him: Whoever claims to live in him must walk as Jesus did."[38] The evidence of our walk in Jesus is our love for one another.[39] Far too many congregations are noted for their ability to devour each other alive. Chewing one another up and spitting each other out, such Christians seem to hold anything and everybody else responsible except themselves.

I am astounded how many pastors I personally know that have been treated in the most unkind fashion by vicious vindictive people who call themselves Christian. This is more than nonsense; this is evil that has worked its way into the fellowship of believers. If Satan masquerades as an angel of light, so do many who pretend to know the Lord, often deceiving even themselves.[40]

James reminds us that what causes fights and quarrels among God's people are the desires that battle within us, in our flesh. When we do not get our way we quarrel and fight instead of turning to God in prayer and trusting in him to supply what we really need.[41] When the flesh motivates, instead of God's love, then the fulfillment of our pleasures have taken center stage. We need to come clean and confess that, too often, we have dumped the frustrations of the flesh on those whose work is to bring us the message of God's love. The pastoral office and those engaged in the work of the ministry ought to solicit the highest of respect; if for no other reason then they have been called by God to serve his Name. The most generous outpouring of love ought to be awarded such representatives of Christ.[42]

However, as dismal as the truth may be, there are far too many church workers who also act contrary to the truth of God's love. Pastors and teachers who are proud and arrogant dictators of their own opinions and like to ride roughshod over those whom they serve are a disgrace to the Spirit of Christ. False servants of Christ are those who convey to others "it's my way or the highway." In actuality, the truth is never "my" way, but always the way of Christ! The message of God is first of all directed towards the messenger. "Therefore, as

God's chosen people, holy and dearly loved, clothe yourselves with compassion, kindness, humility, gentleness and patience."[43]

We should also celebrate, in thanksgiving, the many teachers who faithfully and consistently communicate the love of Christ in educational settings across our land. But, sadly, Christian schools may also be shown to employ teachers who demonstrate anything but positive words of kindness towards their students. At a very impressionable age our children learn in the classrooms to fight for what they cannot have, to shut-up their feelings, to stroke their selfishness, and to stifle their inquisitive questions. The boundaries in which students are frequently taught to operate are inconsistent, unjust, and express favoritism. God spoke against favoritism, "My brothers, as believers in our glorious Lord Jesus Christ, don't show favoritism."[44] If you really keep the royal law found in Scripture, 'Love your neighbor as yourself," you are doing right. But if you show favoritism, you sin and are convicted by the law as lawbreakers."[45] Where is the law of Christ evident in Christian schools that allow cliques, slander, and the ostracizing of peers?

Some churches engage in continual backbiting and tongue wagging. God's Word consistently emphasizes the danger of the tongue in destroying the love of Christ. The number one open door given to Satan to destroy a fellowship of God's people is provided through the mouth. We have been warned by God centuries ago about the destructive power of words. Then, why are so many members of the household of God engaged in gossip and slander of others? God has a lot to say against such love violations.

James instructed, "When we put bits into the mouths of horses to make them obey us, we can turn the whole animal. Or take ships as an example. Although they are so large and are driven by strong winds, they are steered by a very small rudder wherever the pilot wants to go. Likewise the tongue is a small part of the body, but it makes great boasts. Consider what a great forest is set on fire by a small spark. The tongue also is a fire, a world of evil among the parts of the body. It corrupts the whole person, sets the whole course of his life on fire, and is itself set on fire by hell. All kinds of animals, birds, reptiles and creatures of the sea are being tamed and have been tamed by man, but no man can tame the tongue. It is a restless evil, full of deadly poison."[46]

Jesus Christ reminded the church of the priority nature of love when he instructed the church of Ephesus, "Yet, I hold this against you: You have forsaken your first love. Remember the height from which you have fallen! Repent and do the things you did at first. If you do not repent, I will come to you and remove your lamp-stand from its place."[47] And our Savior gave this admonishment after he commended this very same church for her orthodox ways of opposing the wicked and working hard in the church.

Love may cover a multitude of sins, but the lack of love creates endless sins that should not be tolerated in the Church of Jesus Christ. Discernment is needed lest what is called love turns and destroys. The cross of Christ is not only a passionate demonstration of a self-less sacrifice, but offers what humanity needed the most; namely, forgiveness of sins. Christ became incarnate because humanity was enslaved to sin. Faith and love are intricately united in the truth of our Lord. We are driven by our faith to express the love of Christ in the truth. We are motivated by the love of Christ to share the truth of our faith. Truth and love are inseparably connected; one cannot be defined without the other.[48]

Truth void of the love of God is false. Love that communicates what is false is perverted. Faith is grounded in the truth of God's love demonstrated on the cross, while love is an expression of such faith. "And this is his command: to believe in the name of His Son, Jesus Christ, and to love one another as he commanded us."[49] Christ connected obeying the truth with loving others. He taught, "As the Father has loved me, so have I loved you. Now remain in my love. If you obey my commands, you will remain in my love."[50] "My command is this: Love each other as I have loved you. Greater love has no one than this, that he lay down his life for his friends."[51] "This is my command: Love each other."[52]

Any ministry of our Lord that does not prioritize the activities of God's love in Christ has violated the nature of God's indwelling presence. The summary of religion provided through God's servant James has always intrigued me. One would expect such a summary to express some deep theological truth. Actually it does. The awesome truth of God's love in Christ flowing through his creatures summarizes Christianity. James says, "Religion that God our Father accepts as pure and faultless is this: to look after orphans and widows in their distress and to keep oneself from being polluted by the world."[53] In other words, "Attend to the love! Attend to the truth!" As God's love motivates our response, so his love guides our response as well. Christ summed up all that the law of God demands with this one powerful word – LOVE.[54] For God so loved the world that he gave himself in death that we might live in God's love forever.[55]

No-nonsense churches are spread out across our land by the grace of God. These no-nonsense ministries strive, day in and day out, to convey genuine love towards any and everybody they encounter. Pastors, teachers and leaders in the church that sincerely "get it." They understand the priority of love and are motivated by the love of Christ to touch lives and make an eternal impact to the glory of God the Father. No congregation has perfected the expression of love in their midst, but the no-nonsense church possesses the vision of Christ and is compelled by the love of God to serve as his instrument of divine love.

How well are the congregations to which we belong caring for those in distress? We best return to our congregations and review how the awesome power of God's love is living through our churches. We best reevaluate our budgets, activities, decisions and priorities to decipher if indeed the church to which we belong has lost her first love. "For Christ's love compels us, because we are convinced that one died for all, and therefore all died. And he died for all, that those who live should no longer live for themselves but for him who died for them and was raised again."[56]

This is a very anxious world. The many troubles encountered overwhelm and challenge God's people to the max in attending to the downhearted, the poor, and those with special needs. Many are homeless and suicidal. Others in despair turn to inappropriate escapes from their troubles. Still others distract themselves by piling up the things of this world. Everyone is searching for relief. No-nonsense ministries are in the business of providing relief. God said through His apostle Paul, "Carry each other's burdens, and in this way you will fulfill the law of Christ."[57] The no-nonsense church does not reduce the caring for each other to some board or committee. Every member of the Body of Christ has been gifted by God to share the load of loving each other. "Each one should test his own actions. Then he can take pride in himself, without comparing himself to somebody else, for each one should carry his own load."[58]

Often a church's fears prevent love's activities. The church, through her active membership, fears losing members, not making ends meet, or failing in her endeavors. When the ministry is driven by something other than faith, and motivated by a love other than God's love, then the ministry rightfully operates in fear. "It is a dreadful thing to fall into the hands of the living God."[59] The no-nonsense church is motivated by the powerful love of God that drives out all fear.[60] God's love continually brings us back to our roots; namely, an abiding trust in Christ to provide us with all we need for life, now and forever. God's love keeps us ever dependent upon God for the provisions needed to persevere in the faith.

Feeding upon the Gospel of life, we are lifted by God's grace, set on our feet time and again, and empowered to reach out to others as instruments of God's love. God says, "Bear with each other and forgive whatever grievances you may have against one another. Forgive as the Lord forgave you. And over all these virtues put on love, which binds them all together in perfect unity. Let the peace of Christ rule in your hearts, since as members of one body you were called to peace."[61] So "now these three remain: faith, hope and love. But the greatest of these is love."[62] Maybe the late Helen Hayes, considered the first lady of American theater, was correct when she indicated that love is possibly the only glimpse we are allowed into eternity.

There is found no better-written directive for the no-nonsense church of Jesus Christ than the one Paul wrote to the Church at Philippi. He said, "If you have any encouragement from being united with Christ, if any comfort from his love, if any fellowship with the Spirit, if any tenderness and compassion, then make my joy complete by being like-minded, having the same love, being one in spirit and purpose. Do nothing out of selfish ambition or vain conceit, but in humility consider others better than yourselves. Each of you should look not only to your own interests, but also to the interests of others. Your attitude should be the same as that of Christ Jesus."[63] The no-nonsense church responds with a resounding "Amen."

Digging Deeper into the Word of God

1. Read 1 Corinthians 16:22-24. What do you think Paul means when he calls upon a curse to rest on anyone that does not love the Lord? Do you think that Paul would agree that love is the one and only motivator of the Christian life? Do you think Paul would recognize a legitimate love apart from God in Jesus Christ?

2. Read John 15:9-17. Upon what does Christ say his love for God's people is founded? How can Christians remain in the love of Christ? How does obedience result in joy? What is the command of Christ to his people? What is the ultimate expression of love, according to these words of Christ? Jesus, as our friend, laid down his life for us. How does your church sacrifice in her unconditional love for the Savior? Jesus reminds his people that they were chosen by his grace and love. What has God appointed his children to do? What is fruit that will last? How is prayer connected to bearing eternal fruit?

3. Read 2 Peter 1:3-9. Peter reminds God's people that they have freely received from the grace of God in Christ everything they need for life and godliness. What does Peter say to do in light of the precious promises of God? What does Peter say will make Christians effective and productive? The love of God is the pinnacle expression of a godly life in Peter's list of things added to faith. What does Peter mean when he says without these virtues one is nearsighted and blind? How has such an individual forgotten that in Christ he is forgiven?

4. Read Revelation 2:2-5. Why does the Lord commend the Ephesian congregation? What has the church in Ephesus endured? What does Jesus hold against this fellowship of believers? What does the Savior mean by first love? From what height had this church

fallen? What is the Lord's call to this church? What will happen if they do not heed this wake-up call?

5. Read James 2:1-9. What does James say about favoritism? How might this apply to your congregation? How might this apply to any specific fellowship group within your church? In what other ways might favoritism be shown besides the economic one? What proactive means might your congregation use to discourage favoritism? What is the royal law found in Scripture? Why is it called royal? Read Matthew 22:34-40. How is the royal law different then the golden rule? Read Matthew 7:12.

6. Memorize 1 Corinthians 16:14; "Do everything in love."

Endnotes

[1] Heritage of Five Families, 1770-2002, compiled by Vera Emily Suelflow Sweeney, © July 2002, p.58.

[2] Nehemiah 8:10

[3] I John 4:8,16

[4] 1 John 4:10

[5] 1 John 4:11

[6] 1 Corinthians 13:1-3

[7] 1 John 4:19

[8] John 3:16

[9] 1 John 3:14

[10] 1 John 4:20

[11] 1 John 4:14-16

[12] 1 John 4:17

[13] Ephesians 2:5

[14] Matthew 5:44-45

[15] 1 John 3:16

[16] John 15:13

[17] 1 John 3:17-18

[18] James 2:15-16

[19] Matthew 25: 35-36, 40

[20] Matthew 25:40 (see verses 31-46)

[21] Galatians 5:6

[22] Titus 3:2

[23] 1 Peter 3:8-9

[24] 1 John 4:20

[25] 1 John 4:21

[26] Ephesians 4:29-5:2

[27] 1 Peter 4:8

[28] 1 Peter 4:9

[29] Galatians 5:22

[30] 1 Corinthians 13:1-3

[31] 1 Corinthians 13:4-7

[32] Hebrews 10:24-25

[33] 1 Corinthians 12:26 (cf. Ecclesiastes 3:4)

[34] Galatians 5:22-23 (cf. Galatians 5:19-21)

[35] 1 Peter 4:8

[36] John 13:34-35

[37] 1 John 2:15-17

[38] 1 John 2:3-6

[39] 1 John 3:14

[40] 2 Corinthians 11:14

[41] James 4:1-4

[42] 1 Thessalonians 5:12-13

[43] Colossians 3:12

[44] James 2:1

[45] James 2:8-9

[46] James 3:3-8

[47] Revelation 2:4-5

[48] 2 John 1-3 (see verses 4-7)

[49] 1 John 3:23

[50] John 15:9-10a

[51] John 15:12-13

[52] John 15:17

[53] James 1:27

[54] Matthew 22:37-40

[55] John 3:16

[56] 2 Corinthians 5:14-15

[57] Galatians 6:2

[58] Galatians 6:4-5
[59] Hebrews 10:31
[60] 1 John 4:18
[61] Colossians 3:13-15
[62] 1 Corinthians 13:13
[63] Philippians 2:1-5

Chapter 6 – Relationship Oriented
(or "Do I Know You From Somewhere?")

"Therefore, as we have opportunity, let us do good to all people,
especially to those who belong to the family of believers."
Galatians 6:10

I'll never forget Floyd Baker. Floyd walked into my office one day and sat down to chat. He was unshaven and poorly dressed with tattoos quite extensively covering his arms. He did not seem very educated (I found out later he was mildly mentally impaired because of an accident). Floyd was a former hell's angel motorcycle gang member. He had probably taken every drug imaginable. He would say, "You don't want to know what all I've done."

Floyd was one of the most sincere Christians I have met. He knew that he stood out as different from the rest of the membership, but he did not care. He would march himself right down to the front pew where he would sit for worship. He said, "It's time I do things right, I don't care what others think anymore." I easily observed that few knew how to relate to Floyd. Most members were standoffish. I always thought that was nonsense. One of the saddest funerals I have ever conducted was for Floyd, but I rejoiced to know he was with the Lord and no one was looking him over and wondering what he was doing there.

The no-nonsense church, grounded in God's Word, centered in Jesus Christ, empowered by the Spirit, driven by faith and motivated by love is relationship oriented. The essence of life lies in a relationship with God and, consequently, with his people. Expressed not in terms of being acquainted with God, but in terms of intimacy with God. Life does not involve a mere knowing of God but a true "knowing" God in a harmonious relationship of life.

The Biblical account reveals that when Adam "knew" his wife Eve, she bore him a son.[1] The concept of "knowing" in Scripture encompasses the most enduring qualities of an intimate bond between two people.[2] Jesus said, "I know my sheep and my sheep know me."[3] To know God or be known by God is the most precious truth conveyed in the Gospel of our Lord. Such "knowing" expresses the end goal of life.[4]

The devil and his followers know *of* God, but only true believers really *know* God because he has revealed himself in a relationship to them.[5] They have been chosen and sealed by him.[6] God's people belong to God as his adopted children.[7] God is their Heavenly Father, affirmed each time the Lord's Prayer is spoken.[8] The Almighty God invites his people to call him Daddy.[9] The church truly embodies the family of God.

Becoming a member of God's family happens the moment when the living Word of God is implanted in the heart by the power of the Holy Spirit.[10] In that defining moment of conversion a person is transported from death to life.[11] The truest definition of life therefore equals a relationship with God. When Adam and Eve rebelled in the garden and ate of the forbidden fruit they died. And though physical death eventually became an inevitable consequence of their disobedience, it was primarily their relationship with God that received the immediate deathblow.[12] God had clearly warned them, "When you eat of the fruit of the tree of the knowledge of good and evil, you will surely die."[13]

Adam and Eve hid in fear and shame in God's presence, after they disobeyed his Word. God drove them out of the garden. The relationship had changed. The impact of sin brought death to the bond between God and humanity. Though undeserved, God immediately implemented his counter plan to humanity's choice. A plan God had prepared before the creation of the world.[14] God chose to repair the damage caused by man's choice and devised the great plan of salvation before driving man from paradise.[15]

This relationship orientation to true life encompasses more than the bond between man and God. By God's creative act and declaration, the perfected life includes humanity's relationship with humanity. Having created man in God's own image, God determined that it was not good for man to be alone. Not that man was totally alone. Man walked and conversed with God in the garden. And still God concluded that it was not good that man should be left without a "helpmeet," a compliment to his own humanity.

Therein we find not only the institution of the marriage relationship, but also the beginning point of the concept of a family. As God's Word unfolds the history of the human race we find this primary relationship theme of life echoed by our Maker. The entire concept of Israel and the Church is illustrative of God's work of bonding mankind together in the bond they share with their Maker Redeemer.

A Christian's eyes of faith are set upon the true treasures of life. These treasures all express the relationship orientation of life. Faith driven and love motivated, the fruit of God's Spirit ever strives to bond us in love with God and each other.[16] The flow of love from God to man and then returned to God is expressed in man's love, one to another. The stopping of love's flow through man to each other is part and parcel to stopping the return flow of love to God.[17]

Have you ever attended a church's social function? God's people gather for fellowship, fun and friendship. Yet, how many social gatherings have you attended whereby there exists a closed clique over there and another over here and look, there is another one standing off in the corner. And what is happening in these closed groups gathered in the name of Christian fellowship? Very often conversations that speak poorly of others are dominating the topic.

The in-reach focus of the no-nonsense church is concerned with the development of healthy relationships. In the fellowship of believers the church is not intent upon her members bonding around the things of this world, but rather, the things of God. Until we share in the faith, we are not able to fully appreciate the fellowship of earthly things, be it food, fun, sports or other entertaining activities. The goal of in-reach is to bond us in the truth of God's love so that together we might enter the eternal rest in Christ. As the writer of Hebrews directs, "Let us, therefore, make every effort to enter that rest." [18] The no-nonsense church is all about sharing Jesus with others. Why, then, do Christians have such a difficult time sharing God's love? There is as much backbiting, criticizing, bitterness, jealousy and plain 'ole hatred to be observed in the church as outside.

The proclamation of God's love freely given in Jesus Christ is the mission of the church, regardless of how any local congregation might specifically plan to participate in its accomplishment. [19] Though this involves multi-tasks, there is no other purpose for which the people of God gather together in worship and service except to receive and return the love of God in Christ. The no-nonsense church engages in ministry by attending to the relationship opportunities that God gives, beginning with the household of faith.

Christian extremists often ignore the essence of the church's fellowship. Dead orthodoxy is stimulated whenever the dogmatic expression of truth seeks to exclude the "people factor." Liberalism, on the other hand, tends to set aside the truth in order to accommodate people's fleshly desires.

The no-nonsense church recognizes that truth's aim is the impact upon people. "You shall know the truth and the truth shall set you free," our Lord predicted of his disciples. [20] The Gospel of our Lord brings freedom to people from enslavement to self and the flesh. Free to love God and each other. Truth and love are inseparable because truth is expressed in love and love is defined by truth. And they both convey relationship concepts.

This has tremendous implications for the way a church conducts her business. No-nonsense ministries ever remain mindful of the relationship orientation of life. From the way that the ministry is structured to the goals she adopts, the no-nonsense church includes the people factor in all of her strategic ministry plans. Ministry is defined and evaluated in terms of the impact upon relationships. No-nonsense churches are not insensitive to the real relationship needs of her members. Churches characterized as cold to each other, especially to outsiders, exist in violation of their truest identity.

As location is to real estate so relationships are to life. Gary Chapman noted well, "we are relational creatures." [21] Life consists of relationships! Life is expressed in relationships. Life echoes the relationship that the three persons of the Trinity share with each other;

that God shares with man and woman; and that Christ shares with his bride, the Church. All earthly blessings of time, talents and treasures, are simply the resources provided to stroke the true treasure of an intimate relationship with God and His people. This intimacy is conveyed in the promise of eternal life. All gifts of the Spirit have as their purpose to set eyes upon Christ, thereby promoting relationships in the family of God.[22]

Truth is perverted wherever God's people drift from an emphasis on a personal relationship with Christ to a selfish belly gazing operation. Nonsense exists where obsession over gifts, rather than the Giver of all good things, takes root. Abominable nonsense exists whenever God's people, in his name, destroy the relationships that God has established. This is the very reason that Paul admonishes, "Do not repay anyone evil for evil. Be careful to do what is right in the eyes of everybody. If it is possible, as far as it depends on you, live at peace with everyone."[23] The admonishment towards peace is repeated often in the epistles. "Let us make every effort to do what leads to peace and to mutual edification."[24]

God empowers his people to express love with more than words. John writes to his dear friend Gaius, saying, "Dear friend, you are faithful in what you are doing for the brothers, even though they are strangers to you. They have told the church about your love."[25] "God has called us to live in peace."[26] "Aim for perfection, listen to my appeal, be of one mind, live in peace."[27] "Let the peace of Christ rule in your hearts, since as members of one body you were called to peace."[28] "Live in peace with each other."[29] "Make every effort to live in peace with all men and to be holy; without holiness no one will see the Lord."[30]

Peter enjoined the man approved by God; "he must seek peace and pursue it."[31] Christians are peace lovers. Not by setting aside God's Word, but by upholding it. The peace of Christ calls the church into a relationship orientation. God says, "Keep on loving each other as brothers. Do not forget to entertain strangers, for by so doing some people have entertained angels without knowing it. Remember those in prison as if you were their fellow prisoners, and those who are mistreated as if you yourselves were suffering."[32]

The no-nonsense church is relationship oriented and therefore excels in concern for her members. Benevolence is held as an important value to her ministry.[33] In a former congregation that I served, benevolent funding for members was received as a percentage of all offerings. This then was set aside in a special fund account and made available in the church's care for one another. What a blessed way of insuring that the church has funds to appropriately respond financially to any member's legitimate need.

My former congregation also developed a "Love In Action" group effort in responding to the identifiable physical needs of her members. My present congregation responds through an intentional "Crossing Hearts" network of people. Regardless of what a church calls such efforts, the no-nonsense church is intentional about her caring responses. Proactive organized efforts assist the cause to insure that needs are identified and responses are solicited. Time and talent inventories serve to identify the resources available in responding to the struggles, hurts and pains, sufferings and hardships of people.

When a 79-year-old man pulled into a gas station he was immediately surrounded by a group of high school teenagers. Were they going to rob or beat the elderly gentleman? No, just the opposite! More than 300 high school students were given the day off to partake in "Kool to be Kind," charged with performing acts of kindness in a small Wisconsin community.[34] The only thing that seemed wrong with this picture is that no church was involved; this event was created by a public high school.

Why aren't the majority of Christian churches engaged in novel ways to serve others? No-nonsense congregations who operate on the front lines of hands on care come to mind precisely because they are rare. Thank God for those noteworthy congregations engaged in acts of kindness. Why does not every community church make a greater impact on people's daily lives? Churches ought to sponsor events whereby members spread out through the community offering help and assistance to others (i.e. pumping gas, carrying bags, putting bags in cars, sweeping, cleaning, stopping to help wherever help can be had). Small group ministries are excellent resources for community servant events?

God says that every member of the church should have equal concern for each other.[35] Scripture says, "Share with God's people who are in need. Practice hospitality."[36] The no-nonsense church continually evaluates how well she is responding to the body, soul, and spirit needs of her members and beyond. The church should organize her sacrificial responses to God's grace by applying such Scriptural directives, as "do good to all people, especially to those who belong to the family of believers" as we have the opportunity.[37] "Offer hospitality to one another without grumbling. Each one should use whatever gift he has received to serve others, faithfully administering God's grace in its various forms."[38]

Brainstorming sessions ought to frequently stimulate creative and innovative avenues of care. Support groups, teaching opportunities, and hands on labor projects should be ongoing engagements in any ministry. "Love one another" should never be allowed to become a platitude by which the church fails to roll up her sleeves and get to the hard work of actually loving each other. Love is defined in its activities and nothing less (review chapter 5). The no-nonsense church refuses to simply delegate care to any one group, board, committee, or organization. The goal is to develop a culture of caring among the membership. The vision of Christ motivates mindsets, attitudes, priorities, and behaviors towards a relationship responsive climate. Let the church paint vividly the portrait of Christ in the lives of her members. The no-nonsense church prays to be transformed into a vehicle of divine love.

Charity begins at home. Peter echoes Paul when he says, "all of you, live in harmony with one another; be sympathetic, love as brothers, be compassionate and humble. Do not repay evil with evil or insult with insult, but with blessing, because to this you were called so that you may inherit a blessing."[39] Charity extends to the household of God, but does not end at the church's doors. Many churches do a much better job responding to the poor and lost stranger, then caring for their own. Benevolence and charity should remain one of the highest expressions in defining the ministry of Jesus Christ.

Relationship orientation insures the development of a corporate mindset in all decision-making. Not the world's mindset whereby the life of the corporation revolves around the almighty dollar.

The Body of Christ is the sum total of all individual Christians. This relationship orientation of the church serves to prevent the neglect of the few and guard against the favoritism of a minority. Favoritism violates the Body of Christ. James elaborates on this with an illustration, "Suppose a man comes into your meeting wearing a gold ring and fine clothes, and a poor man in shabby clothes also comes in. If you show special attention to the man wearing fine clothes and say, 'Here's a good seat for you,' but say to the poor man, 'You stand there' or 'Sit on the floor by my feet,' have you not discriminated among yourselves and become judges with evil thoughts?"[40]

In some churches the poor are honored and the wealthy professional is the one discriminated against. God's Word nails the issue on the head by viewing any sinful prejudice or arrogant discrimination as a failure to appropriately love others. Paul reminds us, "Do not conform any longer to the pattern of this world, but be transformed by the renewing of your mind. Then you will be able to test and approve what God's will is – his good, pleasing and perfect will."[41]

The oneness of those who belong to Christ is not to be swept aside lightly. Paul says, "so in Christ we who are many form one body, and each member belongs to all the others."[42] As husbands and wives are directed to think in terms of their "oneness," so also the church is guided to strive for oneness in Christ. Speaking against the individualism that plagues our current society, the Body mindset is one whereby every individual is viewed as valuable to the function of the whole. Such unity is not a group fascist mindset whereby the individual no longer counts, only the good of the group.

The unification of God's people is expressed in the analogy of the Body whereby Christ is the head. Within this point of reference, the Spirit of Christ might be viewed appropriately as the heart of the Body. Thus, from the heart of Christ the church receives all gifts that she is to utilize for the common good of the Body.[43] And within this relationship orientation of life in Christ, when one member of the Body suffers, all suffer; and when one member rejoices, all rejoice.[44]

The church has traveled a long ways away from the communal mindset of the early church as recorded in the book of Acts. At that time God's people collectively, "had everything in common. Selling their possessions and goods, they gave to anyone as he had need."[45] In the early church, God's people met no less than weekly for worship. In the context of their weekly gatherings, they shared in the love feasts. Embedded in this forerunner of the potluck supper was the recognition of the divine bond of Christian love. From the very beginning this bond has been threatened by sinful selfish attitudes and decisions. The infamous lies of Ananias and Sapphira gave testimony to the breakdown of selfless service in Christ that resulted in their death.[46] Paul reprimands the church at Corinth for the violation of truth and love in their gatherings.[47]

The no-nonsense church today takes to heart the Word of God in this matter. Recall that the entry of sin into the garden not only separated humanity from its creator, but also brought animosity between each other. Adam and Eve did not enjoy the same intimacy of their relationship after the fall, as before.[48] The first-born son, Cain, kills the second born, Abel, out of jealousy and resentment.[49] This enmity experienced in all relationships because of sin culminated in the sentence of death.

Give thanks to God because Jesus Christ has overcome death on our behalf and brought life and immortality to light.[50] The result of this awesome message of life after death, and intimacy after separation, is the relationship orientation of the Body of Christ. "Therefore encourage one another and build each other up, just as in fact you are doing."[51] "Make sure that nobody pays back wrong for wrong, but always try to be kind to each other and to everyone else."[52]

The no-nonsense church grasps the servant nature of her purpose. She is driven by her faith to wash the feet of others through the forgiveness of sin wrought by the blood of the Lamb. This relationship-oriented life perspective impacts the understanding of ministry. I've noticed that in the last decade, a much greater emphasis is placed on relationships in Christian books. That is great news. Ministries need to adjust their structural realties to convey the truth of this orientation.

Let me illustrate with my own personal ministry acclamations:

A core value held affecting my ministry:
Life is about relationships – period!

First and foremost, my life is about a relationship with God through a personal faith relationship with Jesus Christ. Secondly, my life is about relationships with others. All that God desires from me is summed up in the "agape" word for love. Love God above all, love your neighbor as yourself. Everything else serves as a resource and context by which I attend to relationships, motivated by God's love demonstrated in the truth of Christ.

My personal mission statement:

To use my God-given gifts towards making a genuine positive impact upon others.

My vision of ministry

Flowing from the recognition of my core value is the development and implementation of a relationship-centered ministry that operates around the relationship dynamics between God and people; and people with people. This involves more than mere verbal recognition that ministry is people-centered; something the church has recognized for years.

Stated Goals derived from my ministry vision:

My primary goal involves the minimizing, streamlining, and strategic planning of necessary business matters with the aim to facilitate and encourage the relationship commitments of members to God and each other.

Therefore, I strive to assist the church in moving muscles, where needed…

…away from a program orientation towards a relationship orientation

…away from a business orientation towards a ministry orientation

…away from a results orientation towards a process orientation

…away from a meeting orientation towards a task orientation

...away from a need orientation towards an opportunity orientation

...away from a private orientation towards a corporate orientation

...away from a "get by" orientation towards a "reach your best" orientation

...away from a legalistic orientation towards a grace orientation

...away from a fear orientation towards a faith orientation

Strategic Plan: Three-fold emphasis:
Be in the Word, on your knees, and looking beyond the self!

The Word of God is the means by which God initiates, transforms, and sustains me in a personal relationship with himself. Baptism and the Lord's Supper are connected to the promise of forgiveness in Christ. Worship and Bible Study are essential aspects for a relationship-centered ministry that must solicit my very best resources. Worship involves receiving, celebrating, and sustaining relationships, initiated by God's grace, beginning with God himself.

Prayer is my constant response to the Word of God. A relationship involves good communication, both in listening and talking. Prayer encourages my dependence upon God and keeps me actively involved with what God is personally saying and doing in my life.

Outreach consists of reaching out to others, beginning with my spouse, then proceeding to my children, church family, community and beyond. Much wider then foreign missions, outreach begins at home and stretches as far as the mind can imagine and faith will allow.

Action Plans:
Who, what, when, how,
and where is always a Body/team decision.

I am not alone. I am not an island unto myself. I am not only dependent upon God, but I am in need of others. My mission cannot be fulfilled apart from the Body of Christ

Relationship oriented ministry does not call for business as usual. A dramatic change, in many cases, is necessary to insure that relationships are not treated, at best, as side issues and, at worst, as interference. The establishment of eternal relationships expresses the fulfillment of ministry's objectives.

The "business" of a congregation may inadvertently convey that the attending to relationships is a necessary evil, rather than the call of the church. Certainly a primary reason for this is because many people produce more joy by their exit, then their presence. Members do carry baggage from the past; hurts that have not been healed, anger that has not received proper closure, sins that have not been reconciled. Baggage from the past may not only produce personal interference, but may also interfere in the relationships built around the cross. Unresolved baggage may serve antagonistically against the relationship orientation of the church.

Wherever you have a gathering of sinners you have the potential of conflict. Unresolved conflict between members hinders the building of healthy relationships. Christians may find themselves retreating from the visible Body of Christ due to the vindictive unkindness displayed toward them. When the world offers a peaceful retreat from the chaotic selfishness encountered in the church, then the church has failed miserably in her identity. The no-nonsense church proactively establishes a setting whereby Christians find retreat from the nonsense of the world.

The church's lack of emphasis on relationship building may often be discerned by the way the ministry has been structured. Many churches are organized to be relationship disasters. By their very decisions they exist to divide and distract members from healthy relationship building. We need to reposition our leadership to think in terms of building healthy relationships by every decision made.

Congregations ought to evaluate the way they carry about ministry activities and decisions. Does the ministry promote and build up meaningful connections between members of the church? Does service in the Body of Christ hinder the strength of families or equip family members to fulfill their rolls? Does the church promote intentional building up of one another? Is the encouragement of individual members a priority identified by the stewardship of the

Body? These and similar questions ought to be answered in light of a congregation's activities, structure, and resources.

All of us confuse life at one time or another. Certainly we all have our moments, whereby we participate in the nonsense of the flesh. But, some people seem to live with the aim of complicating life and relationships. Dysfunctional thinking abounds in the games people play. So many hidden agendas and phony masquerades. Why must there be so many crazy-makers in this world? Overly sensitive victims, who incessantly give guilt trips to others, tire out God's servants. People, reacting to underlying feelings that seldom surface in the healthy waters of life, create behaviors putrefied by stinking thinking. Why do internally dying people have to suck the life out of us who desire to truly live?

God-pleasing boundaries provide the safe haven that is needed from the poisonous venom of others. Respected or not, boundaries provide insurance that life given remains the gift the Giver intended for us to enjoy. No-nonsense ministries retain proper boundaries. As difficult as boundaries often prove to be and as evil as they sometimes seem, the real evil is to live without boundaries. "Expel the wicked man from among you."[53] "I urge you, brothers, to watch out for those who cause divisions and put obstacles in your way that are contrary to the teaching you have learned. Keep away from them."[54] Scripture abounds with boundary statements. If the church is to retain her identity and purpose she must attend to the integrity of her boundaries.

Small group ministry, in the last few decades, has risen in popularity largely to meet the relationship needs of the Body. How is the health of such groups? Have they become cliquish and closed groups to outsiders or do they continue to serve by being microcosmic entities of the greater whole? The goal of small groups in the no-nonsense church should seek to remain "Christ Centered, Word Grounded, Faith Driven, Spirit Empowered, Love Motivated, Relationship Oriented," and, as we will discover in the next chapter, "Mission Focused."

Man's highest and greatest musical arrangement does not even come close to expressing the harmony involved in our Redeemer's embrace. To be hugged by God is the ultimate fulfillment of life. For the Almighty to reach down from his throne of power and hold our hand as his very own child provides the absolute pinnacle of security. Augustine said it well; "Our hearts are restless until they rest in you." But, what an understatement!

The fellowship of believers is an extension of fellowship with God. All relationships in the church aim to reflect the relationship of the Body to the Head, Jesus Christ. As my associate once said in a sermon, "We ought to give others a piece of our hearts and not just a piece of our minds." Thank God for those who enter our lives and leave indelible footprints on our hearts. May God bless us so that we might be a blessing to others!

Digging Deeper into the Word of God

1. Read Romans 12:4-5. What does Paul mean when he says the members of the Church belong to each other? In what ways is this inter-connectedness illustrated in your congregation with all of the members? Which members are most likely to feel disconnected with the rest of the membership? What intentional ways does your church sabotage such disconnection?

2. Read 1 Corinthians 12:7-31. How does the comparison of the church to the human body help in understanding the relationship orientation of God's people? In verse 7 Paul says that the gifts of the Spirit are given for the good of all. How effective is your congregation in encouraging everyone to use their gifts for the common good? What does the church need to do in order to solicit the use of all gifts for the good of God's people? Does your congregation have enough roles or avenues to utilize every member's gift?

3. Reread 1 Corinthians 12:26. How does your congregation suffer with those who suffer? In what ways does your congregation rejoice with those who rejoice? What are some innovative ways your congregation could adopt to better attend to the definition of the church as the Body of Christ?

4. Read Colossians 3:12-17. How do these verses illustrate the relationship orientation of God's people? How well is your congregation exemplifying the relationship virtues listed by Paul? Why

is it important to dress our relationship issues in thanksgiving to God through Christ?

5. Read Galatians 6:1-5. Why is it important to admonish our fellow Christians when they are blinded by sin? What do you think it means to exercise gentleness in admonishment? How well does your congregation encourage the sharing of burdens between the members? Why is humility an absolute necessary characteristic of an admonisher? How should the church respond to members who do not pull their own weight?

6. Memorize James 3:17; "But the wisdom that comes from heaven is first of all pure; then peace-loving, considerate, submissive, full of mercy and good fruit, impartial and sincere. Peace-makers who sow in peace raise a harvest of righteousness."

Endnotes

[1] Genesis 4:1

[2] John 10:27

[3] John 10:14

[4] Philippians 3:8

[5] James 2:19

[6] Ephesians 1:17-18

[7] Ephesians 1:5

[8] Matthew 6:9

[9] Romans 8:15

[10] 1 Peter 1:23

[11] Romans 8:1-2

[12] Genesis 3:7-8

[13] Genesis 2:17

[14] Ephesians 1:4

[15] Ephesians 1

[16] 1 Peter 1:22

[17] 1 John 4:7-8

[18] Hebrews 4:11

[19] see chapter 7: "Mission Focused"

[20] John 8:32

[21] Chapman, Gary, The Five Love Languages for Singles, Moody Publishers, c.2004, p.23.

[22] Romans 15:2

[23] Romans 12:17-18

[24] Romans 14:19

[25] 3 John: 5-6a

[26] 1 Corinthians 7:15b

[27] 2 Corinthians 13:11

[28] Colossians 3:15

[29] 1 Thessalonians 5:13b

[30] Hebrews 12:14

[31] 1 Peter 3:11b (cf. Psalm 34:14b)

[32] Hebrews 13:1-3

[33] 1 Timothy 5:3

[34] reported by Roberta Pennington, The Sheboygan Press, October 21,2004, page A2, A4.

[35] 1 Corinthians 12:25-26

[36] Romans 12:13

[37] Galatians 6:10

[38] 1 Peter 4:9-10

[39] 1 Peter 3:8-9

[40] James 2:1-4

[41] Romans 12:1-2

[42] Romans 12:5

[43] 1 Corinthians 12:7

[44] 1 Corinthians 12:26

[45] Acts 2:44-45

[46] Acts 5:1-11

[47] 1 Corinthians 11

[48] Genesis 3:16

[49] Genesis 4:8

[50] 1 Corinthians 15:51-57

[51] 1 Thessalonians 5:11

[52] 1 Thessalonians 5:15

[53] 1 Corinthians 5:13

[54] Romans 16:17

Chapter 7 – Mission Focused
(or "Who Ever Said Bigger Was Better?")

"We are therefore Christ's ambassadors,
as though God were making his appeal through us."
2 Corinthians 5:20

A young mother, stressed out to the max over raising her children and surviving an abusive husband, grabbed a .22 caliber *Saturday Night Special*, aimed it at her head and pulled the trigger. Miraculously, she lived. Her mother-in-law discovered her in the little camper trailer out back in a pool of blood. Her twenty-year-old son was away in the military. Her ten-year-old son and fifteen-year-old daughter would now have to grow up without the care and wisdom of a mother. She would spend the next six months in the hospital and never be the same. Today, the older son provides and cares for his mother. Just as miraculously as the mother who lived, is the son who has grown up to be one of the most faithful Christians I serve. The light of God's mercy and grace shines abundantly all around us.

I had the joy and privilege of baptizing this sixty something mother that only has the mental capacity of an adolescent due to her attempt at suicide. She may not understand much of theology, but one thing she knows for sure - God forgives her in Christ. She loves to look me straight in the eyes and hear me assure her of God's love.

I am reminded of the need to keep the message of Christ simple. This is a good reminder because the church tends to overcomplicate the beauty of the Gospel. As one psychiatrist tells his clients to keep it simple when trying to understand the psyche; so the church ought to guard against overcomplicating the message of the cross.

The mission of the saved is to shine the everlasting light on the Savior. As in pastoral counseling, so in all of the business of the church, God's people need to step back from the growing complications and complexities of ministry and reaffirm the simplicity of her mission. "This little light of mine, I'm going to let is shine, let it shine, all the time, let it shine."

Keeping the message simple does not subtract from the teachings of Christ. Churches overcomplicate the mission by their attempts to manipulate, explain away, change or apologize for the truth revealed in Christ. The mission is simplified by faithful proclamation of the world's Savior, inclusive of the whole truth, and nothing but the truth.

"Lift high the cross of Jesus Christ proclaim, Till all the world adore his sacred name."[1] That is the mission of the church! Keeping the message simple does not reduce this revelation of God to some least common denominator, but rather encompasses all that God has revealed. The focus remains fixated on the sin-payment of the Son of God for the world. Paul says, "We preach Christ, the crucified."[2]

Why does the church remain in this broken world? What captures the ministry's undivided attention? On what is her energy spent? Wherein lies a congregation's passion? What is the goal of the Christian Church? The no-nonsense church exists to be the instrument of God on earth, whereby God's salvation agenda takes preeminence.

God's people are collectively declared to be the "salt of the earth" and "the light of the world."[10] The presentation of God's people as light and salt is engulfed in the whole truth of God. The Great Commission calls upon God's people to present a full disclosure of the truth. The truth brings unity and division. Where light is refused, darkness prevails. Where salt loses its properties, the preservation of the truth is lost. The mission of the church is to present Christ in all of his beauty and truth. Nothing short of teaching everything the Savior commanded his people will accomplish the mission of our Lord. It is his great commission to the church.[11]

The strength of the temptation to reduce or change the message partly lies in the confusion over the church's responsibility. As instruments of the One who came to seek and save the lost, the church is commissioned to be faithful representatives of Christ.[3] God's people are not called to replace the only Savior; they are equipped to represent Jesus through his teachings. Permission to manipulate and culturally assimilate the message in order to make it more palatable to the world is granted in the minds of those who view themselves as responsible to save. There is provided only one Savior. Though the Church's mission may be correctly identified as saving lost souls, God's people best retain the clarity of Paul in understanding that salvation is not accomplished by us, but through Christ, living in us.[4] God makes his appeal through us.[5] Therefore, faithful proclamation to the One is everything to the mission of the Church. The effectiveness of the mission is attributed entirely to God's power, grace, and promises in Christ.

Christians are passionately in love with their Lord. The Body of Christ has been commissioned by him and sent forth into the world as his spokesperson. She is God's embassy on earth. People find refuge in the loving presence of God's people. God's people are the ambassadors of Christ. The church is on a mission for God and nothing shall deter her from its accomplishment. And the mission is to spread the good news of Christ.

The mission is not to bring social injustice to light. The mission is to bring the light of Christ. This mission is not to feed the poor; though attending to the impoverished most definitely engages the heart of the church. Nor is the mission of the church to insure humane treatment of animals, proper stewardship of the world's natural resources, or human rights, though the church is very much concerned about any of these important issues that greatly impact the world in which we reside. The mission is not self-created, but God given.

The Church of Jesus Christ will prevail in her God given mission because the power and presence of God has guaranteed her victory.[6] The Church's triumph does not exclude the reality that individual congregations are in danger of losing their place among the churches of the Savior. The Lord's message to all congregations is the same as given to the church in Ephesus, "If you do not repent, I will come to you and remove your lampstand from its place."[7]

Too many churches spend endless energy greasing the wheels instead of delivering the goods. If a church becomes entangled in the nonsense of fear and doubt, or the distractions of the flesh, then she is in danger of disrupting her mission. When a congregation obsesses over the trivial and argues over the ridiculous, then she endangers the fulfillment of her purpose.

All churches are tempted to avoid the challenging work of sacrificial love. Endless excuses can be heard providing rationales for failing to reach unbelievers with the Gospel. Few ministries are actually willing to roll up their sleeves and aggressively attack the obstacles that prevent effective efforts in impacting lost souls for Christ. I've witnessed too many churches so engulfed in passionate battles for turf and traditions that no energy remains for reaching the lost.

When our younger daughters, Heidi and Holley, were 11 and 9 respectively, we took them to the mall. We were looking at books in the Barnes & Noble when suddenly Kathy and I noticed they were not with us. We looked everywhere. We asked the management, the security guards, and the crowds of people. No one had seen them. I cannot adequately describe the feelings solicited from my belief that our children were kidnapped. I easily imagined the worst. My prayers were intense and demanding. When they were finally found in another store, the joy that came over me was difficult to contain.

If congregations had just a fraction of the concern for the lost that I experienced for our children, then their prayers would be more intensely focused and their activities more determined in seeking and saving the lost. The identifiable problem is not merely a loss of passion for the true mission of the church. The trouble digs deeper into the heart of reality. I'm afraid that if we issued reality checks to all churches they would bounce in the vast majority. For if the truth were known, multitudes of congregations never possessed the passion to reach the lost in the first place. All congregations surely began with the vision of growing and making a difference in the lives of those who stepped into their sanctuaries. But, possessing a firm commitment towards reaching the lost? - seeking and inviting those of a different race or economic status? – such passion never existed from day one in many churches.

How can life long members of a church, worship together, feed upon the Word, year after year, and remain apathetic to the work of the kingdom? People become irate over facilities, what hymns are sung and endless other issues. Let the church report that the support of foreign missions will have to be cut from the budget because of the lack of financial support and the response is as though the church simply announced that the scheduled potluck is cancelled due to a lack of interest.

Our oldest daughter, Jennifer, graduated last year from college. She is pursuing her master's degree. She also wants to take a break and participate in an extended mission opportunity abroad. With the terror and instability of the world today, part of me wants to advise her against a mission trip. On the other hand, part of me wants to shout, "Go for it!" I'm concerned for her safety. I'm more concerned that she lives by faith and not by fear. I'm more concerned that she does not become so wrapped up in this material world that she possesses a false security in life. I'm more concerned about discouraging her from following the call of God upon her life. So I say, "Go for it!"

The same concerns surfaced when our son, Christopher, announced he was joining the army. Knowing that our nation was fighting the war on terror, every fear prompted me to discourage Christopher. But, hearing his passion for becoming an army ranger and listening to his confidence that he believed God was behind his desire made me rethink my response. Christopher had faith that God was with him and that the worse he could imagine was also the best he could imagine, namely, to leave this world and be translated into the very presence of his Savior. So I said, "Go for it!"

Every time the church says no to faith and yes to fear a piece of passion dies until we settle in the doldrums of mediocrity. Christians are found everywhere who faithfully sit in the pews of churches and are anything but fired up to participate in the mission of the church. The call for prayer and service seems to fall on deaf ears with dazed eyes, revealing a depth of boredom unknown in the world of entertainment or sports. The twenty/eighty rule consistently proves true, whereby 20% of Christians support and accomplish 80% of the ministry's work.

The wet blanket of indifference and apathy towards the lost that is cast upon the sunshine of opportunity serves to sober the no-nonsense church. The light of day in the midst of darkness inspires genuine believers to sabotage all attempts that prevent carrying the torch of God's love to the world. The no-nonsense church is passionate about reaching the lost because she is passionately in love with the world's Savior.

I know of a pastor that coveted the professional presence found in the larger churches of the community. He prayed for God to send a professional (i.e. lawyer, doctor, psychologist) to become a member of his church. God answered that prayer. However, he did not anticipate that along with this professional might come a spouse. The manipulation, control, gossip and slander that came forth from that answered prayer taught him a hard lesson. His story reminded me of the movie, "Something Wicked, This Way Comes." In that cinematic production an athlete sells her soul to run again; and runs off insane. The dreams of one after another are granted with a dark and twisted outcome. In the pastor's situation, he should have been praying for God to bring to his congregation the lost, the impoverished and needy of society. Along with them, God would have provided whatever resources he needed to effectively minister. Instead, he prayed for the prestige and resources as an end to themselves. That was a grave mistake.

Not coincidental is God's emphasis throughout the Scriptures upon the widows, orphans, and poor of this world. God has called his people to a life of selfless service. People who are gorging on the fortunes of this world often believe themselves to be self-made and without need. The thirsty ones are searching for true security, the provisions and protection that only God can supply.

Jesus promised, "If anyone is thirsty, let him come to me and drink. Whoever believes in me, as the Scripture has said, streams of living water will flow from within him."[8] Those who are hungry for God are typically those whom the world devalues. They are seeking for the love that only God can supply. The church is the instrument by which God desires to communicate His everlasting love in Christ. "Jesus answered, 'I am the bread of life. He who comes to me will never go hungry, and he who believes in me will never be thirsty.'"[9]

God says, "You are a chosen people, a royal priesthood, a holy nation, a people belonging to God, so that you may declare the praises of him who called you out of darkness into his wonderful light."[12] In the identity of God's chosen people, the church is on a mission to shine the light of Christ in the darkness. In the fulfillment of this mission, the church is to "do everything without complaining or arguing, so that you may become blameless and pure, children of God without fault in a crooked and depraved generation, in which you shine like stars in the universe as you hold out the word of life."[13] The accomplishment of this mission inevitably creates a positive impact upon the society, culture, and community in which she resides. Rather than simply react to the ungodliness of this world, the no-nonsense church is proactive in establishing opportunities for people to retreat from the nonsense into the light of God.

As the church engages in active service to humanity, i.e. feeding the poor, attending to the sick and dying, housing the homeless, protecting the abused, and influencing the market place of ideas and opinions, the light of Christ brings attention to the greater needs of peace and joy in God and the hope of everlasting life. Scripture highlights God's expectation that his people are model citizens, loyal patrons, and trustworthy employees, respectful of authorities and generous to the impoverished and suffering, so as to "put no stumbling block in anyone's path, so that our ministry will not be discredited."[14] Jesus instructed, "Let your light shine before men, that they may see your good deeds and praise your Father in heaven."[15]

The Judeo/Christian worldview, identified with western culture, is fading fast. Though the majority continues to claim Christian identity, their involvement in the gross immorality of the land speaks a different message. How can the citizens of our nation simply sweep away the perversions of the person holding the highest office in our government when he engages in an immoral sexual affair in the White House? And then lies to the American people about it. The surprise does not come from the discovery that the president is a sinner, but from the widespread acceptance of his actions by Christians. Clinton's approval rating, at 65 percent, was higher than any departing president since polling began more than seven decades ago. Is that an expression of forgiveness or a gross toleration of wrong? Maybe the mass excuses offered on behalf of the president sought to provide personal justification for wrongdoing.

The public indifference to morality issues on the part of the Christian community reveals the dawning of a new day. Faster than one can discern, sin is coming out of the closets of mankind and being celebrated. Where is the voice of the churches that supposedly represent the majority of Americans? In the words of my wife's late uncle, "Must it be said again of the watchmen in Zion that they watched but did not see, or they saw but did not understand, or they understood but did not raise the alarm?"[16]

The mission of every individual Christian involves the promotion of healthy relationships in Christ. Sometimes this may seem insurmountable. Specific responsibilities in sharing Christ to significant others are easily confused in the entanglements of the flesh. Dysfunctional power struggles complicate one's mission of proclaiming God's love in Christ.

A woman comes to my office for counseling. She is in her 40s and distraught over her mother who continues the ancient ritual of controlling manipulative selfish behavior. In countless subtle covert and overt behaviors, this mother communicates consistently that she really has no time to engage in this mother/daughter dance, but... And the "but" is always filled with innuendos, deceptive statements, guilt trips and implications that hurt and compound a lifetime of pain. Never does this parent confess to being part of the dysfunction. Throughout the long years of turmoil, never does this parent acknowledge her own sin and self-centered behavior as contributing to the breakdown of the relationship, unless in sarcastic insincere remarks. The nightmare of children who are engrossed in the manipulative, controlling nature of parents is more than a child can bear; even long after childhood has been replaced with age.

As adult children we are in need of boundary clarification. Christians understand the command to "honor our father and our mother." But, just what is our ongoing responsibility in a twisted and perverted parent-child relationship? What should be our response to any relationship that drains the life out of our souls, instead of being life-giving? More specifically to our present topic, "What is an adult child's God-given mission towards a parent who only disrupts the spirit and makes one feel worthless?"

This inquiry brings to light the tension created between honoring a parent and disengagement from victimization. Does a child have any Christian responsibility towards a parent who attempts to entangle her in the nonsense of lies and selfish behavior? Every one of God's children lives in the tension created by the need, on the one hand, for healthy relationships and the sin, on the other hand, which interferes and destroys relationships.

Appropriate healthy relationships may best be discerned by identifying those behaviors that are inappropriate. What is clearly NOT the God-given mission of children is to change or "fix" their parents, because only God is capable of bringing such change. What is equally NOT the God-given mission of the child is to accept or condone or partake of any behavior that is inappropriate and displeasing to God, even though such thinking or acting may be solicited by a parent. To honor our parents does not mean dishonoring our God.

In spite of the challenge presented by a dysfunctional or destructive relationship, the Christian is to retain his/her identity as light and salt.[17] As light, we are always seeking to shine the light on the truth, and as salt, we are always striving to provide enhancement to the reception of the truth. This is often the most difficult towards those relationships that are the closest. The nature of a child/parent relationship brings much baggage to every encounter. A parent's refusal to recognize any self-contribution to the dysfunction of the relationship often results in the necessary creation of a child's distance. Sometimes prayer becomes the only tool available to express love and forgiveness.

Our mission distinctiveness in proclaiming Christ to all must not become lost in relating to others, be it parent or stranger. In other words, others must not be allowed to change the integrity of our truest identity. What is NOT the God-given mission of God's people is to change hearts and souls. Only God can produce such changes. Christians simply serve as catalysts for communicating in word and deeds the message of God. What is NOT the God-given mission of God's people, individually or collectively, is to accept, condone or partake of any thought, word, or deed that is contrary to the love and truth revealed in Christ. Disciples are by definition those who follow, and therefore adhere, to the teachings of Christ.

Faithful adherence to the truth may create division rather than unity, distance rather than closeness. Our challenge is to actually apply the teachings of Christ to all relationships. This is not easy. In fact, this is impossible without the Spirit of God lighting our hearts with the truth of Christ. Jesus taught, "Love your enemies and pray for those who persecute you, that you may be sons of your Father in heaven."[18] "If you love those who love you, what reward will you get?"[19]

Balancing the call to love our enemies is Scripture's warning not to mix inappropriately with the darkness. After reminding the Corinthians that they were ambassadors of Christ, Paul commands, "Do not be yoked together with unbelievers. For what do righteousness and wickedness have in common? Or what fellowship can light have with darkness? What harmony is there between Christ and Belial? What does a believer have in common with an unbeliever? What agreement is there between the temple of God and idols? For we are the temple of the living God."[20] "Therefore come out from them and be separate."[21]

In more than one place, Paul urges the church to "watch out for those who cause divisions and put obstacles in your way that are contrary to the teaching you have learned. Keep away from them."[22] James reminds us that in serving those in need we are to "keep oneself from being polluted by the world."[23] The bottom line is that Christians are to respond to others only to the extent that our Christian integrity of faith remains intact. Otherwise, the fulfillment of our mission is jeopardized.

"In as much as depends on you, strive to live in peace."[24] Living in the peace of Christ requires both an instigator and a responder. When Paul expressed his desire to become all things to all men in hopes that they might be saved, he was not advocating throwing integrity out the window.[25] He was promoting the meeting of others on their own turf. Christians seek to befriend prostitutes, not become a friend of prostitution. We desire to befriend the homosexual, not homosexuality; the alcoholic, not alcoholism; the selfish, not selfishness, those who live in this world, not the world itself.[26] The church seeks to embrace the impoverished, not poverty. We are ambassadors of Christ as though God were making his appeal through us. His appeal to be reconciled to God through his Son, Jesus Christ.[27]

The no-nonsense church passionately prays to be used by God to win others to Christ. The faithful conveyance of the love of Christ is withheld from no one. The church needs to keep in mind that many reject the love of Christ. Jesus said, "Do you think I came to bring peace on earth? No, I tell you, but division. From now on there will be five in one family divided against each other, three against two and two against three. They will be divided, father against son and son against father, mother against daughter and daughter against mother, mother-in-law against daughter-in-law and daughter-in-law against mother-in-law."[28]

All nations, tongues, and people are the objects of the Church's mission, albeit, apart from the integrity of true faith, the mission cannot be accomplished. The same holds true for the parent/child relationship or any other relationship opportunity to share the message of reconciliation. To drop integrity in order to accomplish the mission is disastrous. Tantamount to using a flashlight with a weak battery is the person who attempts to make the message palatable to the world of nonsense. By the time the mission is delivered, the message has become so diluted with man's wisdom that there is no distinctive taste left. The salt has lost its saltiness. Jesus said, "If the salt loses its saltiness, how can it be made salty again? It is no longer good for anything, except to be thrown out and trampled by men."[29] Weak, dim light can hardly light the way.

Christian nonsense is often responsible for the church's message being thrown out and trampled upon by the world. Christ said, "Do not give dogs what is sacred; do not throw your pearls to pigs. If you do, they may trample them under their feet, and then turn and tear you to pieces."[30] In order to fulfill the church's mission we are to, first of all, heed the Scripture's call to truth. "So then, just as you received Christ Jesus as Lord, continue to live in Him, rooted and built up in Him, strengthened in the faith as you were taught, and overflowing with thankfulness. See to it that no one takes you captive through hollow and deceptive philosophy, which depends on human tradition and the basic principles of this world rather than on Christ."[31]

In spite of the world's rejection, the church remains focused on her mission. The mission explains why God has left us on this broken planet. Surely we are not left behind as some sick joke. As Paul concludes, "I desire to depart and be with Christ, which is better by far."[32] But, here we are. The Savior's Great Commission given to His people provides the mission of the Body of Christ. Our Lord commanded, "Go and make disciples of all nations."[33] This of course begins at home, in the home. The focus to share God's love extends from the home to the household of God and beyond.[34]

Motivated by God's love, the heart of the church is dedicated to reach others for Christ. Paul instructs, "Be wise in the way you act toward outsiders; make the most of every opportunity. Let your conversation be always full of grace, seasoned with salt, so that you may know how to answer everyone."[35] The aim of the mission is always to be effective instruments of light in making disciples of Christ.

In the last twenty years or so the Church Growth Movement has inundated the church with inspirational material challenging God's people to prioritize the Great Commission. Multitude of churches have renewed their commitments and rearranged their polity to better focus on the church's mission of sharing the Gospel of Jesus Christ with the world. Excellent! Yet, still the observation is easily made that the vast majority of churches remain mesmerized with navel gazing.

The church's ministry involves two aspects of reaching people; namely inreach and outreach endeavors. We are commanded, "And let us consider how we may spur one another on toward love and good deeds. Let us not give up meeting together, as some are in the habit of doing, but let us encourage one another – and all the more as you see the Day approaching."[36] The church gathers in worship primarily to receive from God's hand of grace all that is needed for forgiveness, life and salvation. Bible study is imperative for fanning the flame of faith. We are instructed to build ourselves up in the most holy faith.[37] The point of all in-reach is to equip the saints for the work of the Lord.[38] And the focus of kingdom work ever remains on the Great Commission to go forth into the world and make disciples of all people.

The proclamation of Christ is the highlight of our present reality on earth. What other reason has the Lord left us in this veil of tears? Why doesn't God translate us immediately to our home above where all suffering, pain, sorrow, grief, tears and troubles are removed from our experience?[39] The reason the Lord has not ended our earthly journey, both as individuals and as a church, is that there are yet others to become disciples. Christ said, "And this gospel of the kingdom will be preached in the whole world as a testimony to all nations, and then the end will come."[40] All believers are God's chosen instruments to get the job done. God, by his grace, invites and enables his people to participate in the saving of souls, a job he could jolly well accomplish without us.

Secured in Christ through forgiveness from all sin, we discover our value. We discover meaning and purpose. In Christ, we are valued as ambassadors of the Lord.[41] God has a plan to use us, not because he is dependent upon us, but in order that we might discover the joy of our dependency in serving him. Christ has created us for such a day.[42]

Spirit-filled leaders who are mission focused lead no-nonsense ministries. No-nonsense leaders realize that the opportunities and needs of ministry are unlimited, unlike the ministry's resources. They are disciplined in their ability to selectively say no to the never-ending requests that may present themselves in order to utilize the available ministry's resources. Christian leaders are also constantly asking and seeking for God's open doors to provide testimony to the Gospel of Christ.

The open doors provided, as well as the closed doors encountered, for fulfilling the Great Commission continually challenge the church to remain dependent upon God. Living by faith requires the church to remain on her knees, asking and seeking God's will in fulfillment of her mission. Rather than simply reacting to the loudest voices or to special interest groups or the first opportunity that presents itself, healthy ministries strive to be prayerful, proactive, and contemplative in utilizing the gifts of God's grace.

The ministry that is focused on her mission is clear about the purpose for which God has called her into existence. She is constantly seeking greater clarity on the unique details of answering God's call. The larger a ministry grows in opportunity and resources the more complex it becomes. This complexity of ministry requires a concise clarity on a congregation's identity and purpose. To the extent that a congregation is unclear in understanding how she is differentiated from the world and other congregations, she will falter in the task of prioritizing opportunities and resources to fulfill her purpose.

No-nonsense ministries realize the need to keep constantly before their membership the "born anew" status, by which God's people become servants of the living God. Until we inwardly digest that we are only strangers here, heaven is our home, we will fail to become the living stewards that we confess to be. Peter writes his first epistle to "God's elect, strangers in the world."[43] Paul reminds us to "Set your hearts on things above, where Christ is seated at the right hand of God. Set your minds on things above, not on earthly things."[44]

Prayerful engagement of resources creates the need to exercise continual evaluative decision-making in regards to ministry activities. Yesterday's needs may no longer be the priority of today. What has been effective in the past may have ceased its effectiveness in today's changing culture. The no-nonsense church is not locked in to former decisions, stuck in a rut, or framed by the past. Needs arising in the present may not have been recognized in the days gone by. Always listening to the call of God, ever responding in prayer, and persistently looking beyond herself, the church focused on the truth of Christ seeks to ascertain her resources for ministry and to respond with a clear mission vision.

This prioritizing of needs is easier said than done. And once done, the importance of prioritizing continues to call the people of God into the process of evaluative decision-making. No-nonsense ministries do best to setup a "think tank" process whereby they carefully and intentionally call into question the effectiveness of any and all areas of ministry. The no-nonsense church is continually brainstorming new and creative responses to identified needs and opportunities. This "think tank" should consist of leaders who have shown a high commitment to and understanding of the mission of the congregation. These leaders should have also demonstrated a high level of personal commitment to the ministry in which they are engaged. And, of course, those gathered to strategize the mission's vision should be entrenched in the study of God's Word.

I believe the visionary pastor of the congregation best leads this "think tank" cadre of leaders. The pastor designated to carry the torch, set the vision, and clarify the mission, is preferably freed from most other responsibilities except preaching and teaching. This is necessitated in order to maintain the strength of focus upon evaluative brainstorming of the ministry's effectiveness. The pastor often becomes bogged down with excessive administrative needs. This robs the pastor of the strength of mind to spend in contemplative reflection on the mission effectiveness of the ministry. The early church's example of insuring that the spiritual leaders of the church remained focused in the Word and prayer has been cast aside far too frequently by congregations as impractical idealism.

One of the main obstacles in allowing the pastor adequate time to focus on "Word and prayer" ministry involves the lay membership's attitude. Lay members may convey that the pastor's time spent in prayer and study of God's Word is not acceptable. Lay leaders do not outright suggest this concept. That would be too blatant in opposition to the value of the Word proclaimed. No, this mindset is usually conveyed in countless criticisms, verbal suggestions and implications, as well as expectations that simply require a different focus of the pastor's time. The no-nonsense church intentionally protects the value of having her pastors prioritize Word and prayer activities.[45]

Every endeavor and activity of the ministry ought to be annually evaluated in its relationship to the fulfillment of the mission. Recurrently, the adopting of congregational budgets reveals that this annual exercise primarily concerns whether or not there is sufficient money to rubber stamp the status quo. Seldom is there a felt freedom to analyze whether a particular aspect of the budgeted ministry should continue to be supported.

Congregations find it much easier to add than subtract from the supported ministry endeavors. The main reason for this reality is the difficulty that discontinuing any ministry activity involves. Even though it may not be the most effective or the best stewardship of the congregation's resources, once begun the detrimental impact of ceasing a certain endeavor is usually avoided, sometimes at ridiculous costs to the fulfillment of the ministry's goals.

Ideally, every board, committee, task force, any endeavor or activity, all organizations connected to a ministry are annually scrutinized in light of the congregation's mission vision. The question analyzed is not reduced to whether a particular aspect of ministry is connected to the mission, but the more meaningful question proposed is, "Might there be a better way to organize or use our resources to accomplish our stated purpose?" No-nonsense ministries are dead set upon the fulfillment of their mission and are willing to make any necessary adjustments in order to enhance the effectiveness and success of their identified reason for existence.

The implementation of recommendations to discontinue long standing activities or groups will most likely irritate those invested in such endeavors. Regardless, the no-nonsense church is relentless in prioritizing the mission while exercising good stewardship of her resources for such accomplishment. When having to deal with staff reduction, no-nonsense ministries strive to communicate well to all involved the necessity and the desirability of reallocating the limited funds available. No-nonsense ministries engage in ongoing, above board, education that prepares leaders for expectant evaluations. Members invested in any particular endeavor are specifically solicited and encouraged to take ownership of the necessary evaluation process leading to appropriate mission-focused decisions. The object is not to reduce ministry, but to insure that the congregation is putting her best foot forward in meeting stated objectives.

I observe that one of the reasons there exists so much apathy among the members of a church in answering the call to serve is that many of the congregation's activities are perceived as trivial or ineffective. People want to serve in ways that have clear correlations to the meeting of set goals. Time is just too precious of a commodity in everyone's life to offer it frivolously or without clarity of purpose.

I further observe that for a congregation to get excited about new possibilities in accomplishing her mission, the congregational leaders model such excitement. This clearly includes the paid ministry staff. Often an individual lay member may initiate mission enthusiasm by stimulating a new open door of ministry opportunity. How well such new endeavors will be received and supported by the congregation typically depends upon the endorsement and excitement exhibited by the leadership (paid and volunteer). The same typically holds true for the church's direct involvement in mission work. Every leader ought to be regularly encouraging members to support the outreach efforts of her mission. Personal involvement in sharing the love of Christ has no replacements. All of God's people are called to testify to the truth of Christ.

The story of a young Russian girl provides an inspiring illustration of the beauty and challenges experienced on the mission field. Olga would never be the same again. Her life encountered a love that she had never known before. She was overwhelmed by the willingness of our daughter's friendship. Awe-struck by the genuine intensity of sincere compassion, Olga was clueless in how to respond. How could she adequately express the impact upon her spirit from her brief encounter with Jennifer? Less than two weeks prior they had met for the first time.

Inspiring stories are multiplied across the globe many times over as short-term mission teams are commissioned by congregations and sent across the globe to share the love of Christ with strangers in foreign lands. Hundreds, thousands, of churches annually respond with enthusiastic teams sent to penetrate the darkest nights of this world. The no-nonsense church desires to dig deeper into the reality of her mission involvement. The sunshine of short-term mission trips aims at more than superficial or temporary effectiveness. God's power brings everlasting change as his plan of grace unfolds.

Acknowledging God's awesome oversight does not provide the no-nonsense church with an excuse for failing to utilize her resources to accomplish long-term objectives. The no-nonsense church prays for follow-up opportunity in the lives they have touched. Excitement abounds when one brings God's love to others. To haphazardly abandon the light that now shines in a new heart is unthinkable. The most heart-rending experience of short-term mission work is the unavoidable retreat from the seed planted by God's Spirit, knowing that the poisonous darkness still encamps around the new Christian. In the absence of Christian fellowship and encouragement, the future looks bleak. Only the miracle of God's provisions will insure the permanent value of love shared. The starkness of leaving the mission field and returning to the comforts and safety of home serves to sober the faithful while humbling God's servant.

The no-nonsense church engaged in accomplishing her mission will anticipate the inevitable impermanence of her involvement. She will continually strive to develop an ongoing impact upon the lives touched. For instance, Olga is a brand new teenage Christian who resides in the absence of nurturing Christian relationships. Engrossed in poverty with no Christian friends, no Christian parents, and no prospective Christian husband, her fate appears quite dark. This all too real scenario is what rips apart two hearts bonded in Christian love as their brief earthly journey now experiences the pain of separation.

The tragedy of separation is intense. The encounter had revealed what life could be, was intended to be, but is not to be. The answer to this tragedy should not lie in the willing retreat of the church. Scripture warns that when demons are cast out they return with reinforcements.[46] The church has ongoing obligations and responsibilities to pray for and remain alert to further open doors of service to those they have impacted. The no-nonsense church seeks intentional follow-up in her mission endeavors, be it locally or abroad. I have always been impressed with the U.S. Army's motto: "No one left behind." The no-nonsense church has the same attitude. Too many mission endeavors remain on the surface of superficiality, only engaging the church in the pretense of making a lasting difference.

Before a mission team ever enters the battleground they should commit to forming eternal relationships. Each participant should be in prayer that God might enable him or her to form a lasting bond with at least one person. Even before stepping onto the front lines of service, a person should anticipate the inevitable good-byes involved and have already formulated a plan to maintain ongoing communication and friendship whenever possible. The plan ought to consider provisions for continual support. In this way we seek to honor the bond that God has created in Christ and surely God will bless such efforts.

A vital question remains continually before all churches, "Just how well are we doing in remaining focused on the mission at hand?" Surveys may assist a congregation in gathering the necessary data to answer this question. The personal one on one, face-to-face, interviews with those who are impacted by the various aspects of the ministry will always provide a more effective discernment of the truth. At the least, a random sampling of personal testimonies ought to reveal interesting insights into a ministry's impact.

The no-nonsense church welcomes, rather than fears, personal feedback, input, and appropriate suggestions concerning her effectiveness. She is not immune or oblivious to such critical testimonies and seeks to implement whatever legitimate changes might improve the fulfillment of her mission. The no-nonsense church not only welcomes, but also humbly accepts appropriate feedback as part of her identity as an imperfect church.

God has given a mission to his Church. No-nonsense ministries sincerely desire to know when their attempts to reach out with the love of Christ are counter productive. They prayerfully accept accountability for remaining mission focused.

Christians continue to walk on planet earth because they have a job to do and when the task is complete they will no longer walk this boulevard of broken dreams. On their own, they are ill equipped and completely incapable of fulfilling the mission. Secure in Christ, grounded in God's Word, empowered by God's Spirit, driven by faith, motivated by love and bonded in eternal relationships, God's people are fully equipped to realize the significance of accomplishing their God-given mission. The no-nonsense church will always remain mission focused.

Digging Deeper into the Word of God

1. Read James 5:19-20. How much energy should the church place on reclaiming those who have "dropped out" of the church? What does James mean by covering over sins? Compare this to 1 Peter 4:8-10. How is your church seeking to turn the sinner from his sinful ways? Is it appropriate to call one to faith without calling him or her to repentance? Read Acts 2:38-39.

2. Read 1 Peter 3:13-17. No one desires to suffer. Why should the prospect of suffering not prevent us from sharing Christ with

others? Why is it important to grace our testimonies with gentleness and respect? In the final declaration Peter seems to anticipate that a person's Christian testimony might be rejected. Should the suspicion that your testimony might be rejected prevent you from giving it? Why or why not? What is the most effective way to be prepared to give testimony to the truth?

3. Read Hebrews 13:2. What do you think this means? How might this color the way we approach the lost among us? Do you think you have ever encountered an angelic visitation? How might this influence the way you respond to visitors attending your congregation?

4. Read Colossians 4:5-6. How is your congregation considerate of others without compromising the truth? How is your church making the most of every opportunity? How are opportunities identified, promoted, and supported? Think of practical illustrations that show the meaning of verse 6.

5. Read Ephesians 5:15-16. What is Paul warning Christians about in their outreach endeavors? Do you think the present days are more, or less evil, than in the days of Paul? How does your congregation equip her members to fulfill Paul's directives in these two verses?

6. Memorize 1 Peter 3:15, "But in your hearts set apart Christ as Lord. Always be prepared to give an answer to everyone who asks you to give the reason for the hope that you have. But do this with gentleness and respect."

Endnotes

[1] Kitchin, George W., "Lift High the Cross," (Hope Publishing) 1827-1912, used by permission.
[2] 1 Corinthians 1:23
[3] Matthew 5:13-14
[4] Matthew 28:18-20

[5] Luke 19:10; Matthew 28:20

[6] compare 1 Corinthians 9:22 with 10:33 (cf. Galatians 2:20)

[7] 2 Corinthians 5:20

[8] Matthew 16:18

[9] Revelation 2:5c

[10] John 7:21

[11] John 6:35

[12] 1 Peter 2:9

[13] Philippians 2:14-16a

[14] 2 Corinthians 6:3

[15] Matthew 5:16

[16] Suelflow, Roy, <u>Christian Churches in Recent Times</u>, Concordia Publishing House: Saint Louis, Mo., c.1960, page 228.

[17] Mathew 5:13-16

[18] Matthew 5:44

[19] Matthew 5:46

[20] 2 Corinthians 6:14-16a

[21] 2 Corinthians 6:17a

[22] Romans 16:17

[23] James 1:27

[24] Romans 12:18

[25] 1 Corinthians 9:19-23

[26] James 4:4

[27] 2 Corinthians 5:20

[28] Luke 12:51-53

[29] Matthew 5:13

[30] Matthew 7:6

[31] Colossians 2:6-8

[32] Philippians 1:23

[33] Matthew 28:19

[34] Galatians 6:10

[35] Colossians 4:5-6 (cf. Ephesians 5:15-16)

[36] Hebrews 10:24-25

[37] Jude: 20

[38] See 2 Timothy 3:16-17

[39] Revelation 7:15-17

[40] Matthew 24:14

[41] 2 Corinthians 5:20
[42] Ephesians 2:8-10
[43] 1 Peter 1:1
[44] Colossians 3:1-2
[45] see chapter 9
[46] Like 11:24-26

Chapter 8 – Generosity Exemplified
(or "What Have We Become?")

"You will be made rich in every way
so that you can be generous on every occasion,
and through us your generosity will result
in thanksgiving to God."
2 Corinthians 9:11

The first real encounter I had with one of the congregation's life-long members was in a quaint little restaurant where my wife and I were dining with some friends. His reputation had preceded him. He was known for his boisterous opposition to the dreams of the church. When he saw us he marched right over to the table where we were sitting and in a loud obnoxious tone of voice, as if to call the attention of everyone present, he introduced himself, followed by a firm declaration, "You don't know me but I will say one thing, don't ever expect me to give any money. I'll come to church, but don't ask me to give, I just don't do that." These may not have been the exact words used, but his message was delivered with absolute clarity.

Something else became crystal clear – this member did not possess the gift of generosity![1] The Spirit of God was not prompting him to make such a firm declaration to his new pastor. How can a child of grace be so adamantly against the call to give, even boastful about his miserly refusal to consider contributions to the work of the Lord?

Increasingly, since the Industrial Revolution societies have become confused about the differentiation between needs and desires. In the western cultures of the world, the line drawn between the two have become ridiculously blurred. From cell phones, to laptops, to Hummers and SUVs, to big screen TVs and Ipods, the average American citizen actually believes these are his entitlements to a good life.

The arrogant attitude, that Christians have somehow earned the blessings of God or have a right to them, is offensive. Worse yet, I know Christians who say, "God did not help me get what I have, why should I give him anything now?" Few are so blatantly conceited. The few may be the loudest, most powerful and influential voices in our congregations. God help our churches if they are. The no-nonsense church condemns all such arrogance.

Americans are overwhelmed by the availability of worldly things. Constantly bombarded by seductive advertisements to own yet one more toy or gadget, those who are without yearn to possess the latest and the greatest that technology has produced. Western culture is suffocating from over exposure to the things of this world. The plethora of products that beckons to the consumer creates the illusion that more is better. We live in what others have called a world of purchase. The world beckons to meet our insatiable appetites. Easy credit calls out for us to buy yet that one more thing we need in order to realize happiness.

In this world of endless neediness the church abides. Unless she is absolutely centered in Christ and clarified on her purpose, she will fall into the deceptive traps of materialism set by the devil. I was recently assisting our oldest daughter in buying a car. No matter how hard we tried, we found it impossible to get a salesman to give us the bottom line price upfront. Confusing us with trivial information impertinent to our desired purchase and going back and forth to the manager, the plan sought to wear us out and totally confuse us so that we loss the integrity of our original buying parameters. The wisest car buyer enters the purchasing arena with a firm financial boundary.

The stewardship wisdom of the Bible underscores the same. Up front, as first fruits, one makes a decision to give a set percentage of one's income so that when the endless "needs" and possibilities are presented – the decision to buy operates within the spending limits already determined by the set giving parameters. Otherwise, in the confusion of materialistic desires, giving may be reduced to what is leftover. Generosity then is defined in terms of feeding the self.

The sinful and unclean heart, impoverished by the flesh, reveals the desperations of the soul. We are poor miserable sinners drowning in a sea of selfishness. We are forged in the fires of worldly nonsense, vomiting voluminous words of stinking thinking The sinful flesh is so warped that, even in our rebirth, we are enticed to cling to our old identities. Paul confesses, "For what I want to do I do not do, but what I hate I do. And if I do what I do not want to do, I agree that the law is good. As it is, it is no longer I myself who do it, but it is sin living in me. I know that nothing good lives in me, that is, in my sinful nature."[2]

Paul further reflects, "So I find this law at work. When I want to do good, evil is right there with me. For in my inner being I delight in God's law; but I see another law at work in the members of my body, waging war against the law of my mind and making me a prisoner of the law of sin at work within my members. What a wretched man I am!"[3]

God's people find it very difficult to listen to Biblical teachings on the subject of financial management, much less apply the principles taught. Everything in our flesh, in our sinful nature, cries out against the concept of generosity. Born of the flesh, we are enemies of God's nature.[4]

Where God is love, we by nature tend towards hate. Where God is giving, we are selfish. Where God is just and righteous, we are poor miserable sinners. Only in the power of the living Spirit of Christ are we recreated in the likeness of God. Having been reborn, our flesh continues to gnaw away at our new way of thinking, corroding our trust in God's Word, and sabotaging any application of God's revelation.

God must shed tears over the selfish responses of those who encounter his grace and mercy. The pervasive lack of trust in God is especially evident in the financial management and giving habits of those who claim to give their first allegiance to the Lord Jesus Christ. The sinful flesh persistently convinces God's people to believe that they somehow deserve the blessings of grace they so freely enjoy.

Sin is the great separator of man from God. And Christ is the Prince of Peace, recreating us in the bond of peace. Having redeemed us from sin, death, and the devil, Christ is forever uniting us in harmony with God, our Father, through faith. This incomprehensible and totally undeserved exchange of death and life is the one and only proper motivator of our giving response. Biblical stewardship is nothing less and nothing more than the response of God's people to the love of God revealed in our hearts.[5] Jesus said, "Freely you have received, freely give."[6] The only appropriate response to the reception of God's gift of life is the proper management of life given.

Life management is all-inclusive. Every gift of time, talent, and treasure, every opportunity, every relationship is viewed under the scrutiny of faith in Christ. Deep within one's soul, a God created attitude change propels those born anew towards an all-encompassing dependent relationship of trust. No-nonsense Christians recognize that all material blessings are resources provided to serve their relationship with God.

In the whole world over, the majority of Christians everywhere, in all denominations, seem to struggle in adhering to the Biblical principal of generous first fruits proportionate giving. The true test of living by faith in the Son of God cannot be separated from how believers use the resources bestowed upon them by a gracious forgiving God. The Christian's faith determines his/her priorities. How could it be otherwise?

Our Lord had much to say on the subject of attachments, or lack thereof, to the things of this world. The majority of all that Jesus taught were directly related to the handling of our material possessions. Our Master Teacher is the one who underscored the subject of stewardship in the life of his followers. The radical nature of living by faith defies the mathematical reasoning of saving and hoarding the blessings of God. The Lordship of our Savior brings to our inner most beings a peace that is beyond all human understanding and a joy that knows no end.[7] God loves a cheerful giver precisely because such a person is operating in the freedom of faith. The call of faith is nothing less than total dependency upon God for life.

God extends, through His prophet Joel, the invitation for his children to return to him with a devoted heart. "Rend your heart and not your garments," the Lord entreats his people. "Return to the Lord your God for He is gracious and compassionate, slow to anger and abounding in love, and he relents from sending calamity."[8] "Who knows? He may turn and have pity," Joel declares. God may leave behind a blessing. What does the inspired prophet suggest this blessing will be? "Grain offerings and drink offerings for the Lord your God."[9] God blesses the life of repentance and faith with the resources necessary to give back to the Lord. The real prosperity of earthly life is the privileged opportunity to serve the Lord.

I recently met a Christian who inspired me. He shared with me how he was blessed with a ministry to prisons. "Is this a volunteer ministry?" I inquired. "Yes," he replied. "And I'm about to be blessed with a ministry to the homeless." How rare for church members to voice the giving of their time, talents, and treasures as a welcomed blessing of the Lord.

Living free from the enslavements of the self is one of the most difficult tasks in this world. Equally difficult is making idols out of the things that money can buy. Since money is often viewed as the culprit preventing one's happiness, the almighty dollar easily replaces the Almighty. God says, "Keep your lives free from the love of money and be content with what you have, because God has said, 'Never will I leave you; never will I forsake you.'"[10] The church, made up of the likes of us, is definitely not immune to the money pressures and materialistic desires of the flesh. Where sinners are gathered there exists the lust for money. The no-nonsense church is not immune to the temptations of the flesh as it relates to the material world.

Confident trust on the part of God's people rests entirely upon the awesome promise of the Gospel. "If God be for us, who can be against us?"[11] At the heart of Christian living is the flesh defying, logic denying, faith in God's provisions for a life of security and significance. Paul reminds us, "Whether we live or die, we belong to the Lord."[12]

Judas Iscariot had every advantage. He had a loyal band of friends. His personal teacher was the Lord of the universe. Did Jesus designate Judas as treasurer to assist him in overcoming his weakness? One thing is obvious in the Biblical record – the selfish nature got the best of Judas. Judas became the infamous traitor of the world's Savior.

The end of the betrayer's life is marked with despair and suicide. God informs us that he went out and hung himself.[13] Every Christian has surely at one time or another dreamed or imagined what it would have been like to meet Jesus Christ personally in the flesh. How could a personal companion of our Lord betray him? The Bible informs us that Judas loved money.

Now if the love of money can infiltrate the spirit, destroy the life, and damn the soul of one of the apostles, surely the church should sit up and pay attention. Paul warned Timothy that the love of money was a root for all kinds of evil.[14] Before we get feathers ruffled because our pastors mention the unpopular church word – MONEY, we should understand what is at stake – our eternal welfare. Do you recall the story of the Rich Fool? [15] Jesus pulled no punches and made no bones about the dangers of money. The Bible warns repeatedly that misdirected devotion to material wealth destroys life. Jesus hammered home the dangers involving worldly possessions.

The church should unashamedly exhort the people of God to keep their lives free from the love of money. The love of money is revealed by God to be a satanic trap. Judas is a vivid reminder of that fact. His love for money literally opened up his life for Satan to enter and destroy.[16] Let God's people learn his lesson well and apply it in the life of the church.

Jesus did not call the church to live free from the use of money. His band of disciples obviously had a treasurer and a treasury. Jesus accepted the generosity of many people and taught his disciples to do the same. [17] God did not advocate the life of poverty for its own sake. He never said we should refuse all money or goods in life. God set up clear provisions for the financial stability of his people organized in the Old and New Testaments.

On the other hand, Christ did make it emphatically clear that our dependency should be, not upon the things of this world, but upon our Heavenly Father who owns it all. We are reminded repeatedly that God will take care of our every physical need as we trust in him and use our blessings according to his divine principles. We are called to be totally devoted to our Lord. Jesus warned about the dangers to the soul in forgetting the source of earthly blessings. Genuine believers live lives of thanksgiving for the blessings enjoyed. Money is perceived as a resource in the life of faith.

A perverted handling of our money and goods occurs whenever we turn our trust away from God and place our confidence on the accumulation of material wealth, power or fame in order to satisfy our identity crises. Created things cannot possibly fulfill our security and significant issues! We search in vain for meaning in life apart from the purpose for which we were created and redeemed. We handle the things of this world in vain apart from the purpose for which earthly possessions are given.

The flesh is entirely incapable of keeping the proper focus on the things of this world. Only in the Spirit of God are we provided with a new vision, a new identity out of which proper life management is possible. From the time we could walk and talk we have been in search of the answer to the question, "Who am I?" And in every stage of life we revisit this question. Pre-adolescence, adolescence, teenage, graduation of high school, entering upon a career, marriage, midlife, and retirement, each and every stage brings the question back to the forefront of life.

As does every major change or loss in life; each change of circumstance such as the death of a loved one, divorce, unemployment, loss of health, or change of career brings the formative quest for identity to mind. We are forever seeking the answer to our identity question. We are on a life-long mission to find ourselves. And just when we begin to rest secure in the answer we have drummed up, something shakes the foundation. If our identities are drawn from our employments, then when we lose our jobs through being fired, laid off, loss of health or retirement we no longer know who we are. Our identity is in crises. Same thing happens if we draw our identity from our spouses and they die or divorce us. Or, if our identity is dependent upon our children and one of them is lost, then our identity melts away like the wicked witch of the East in the Wizard of Oz.

Only our Maker/Redeemer is capable of instilling within us a true and firm identity. Having created and recreated us in his love, God is the potter and we are the clay. He knows how and why he made us. He alone is able to establish us in an identity that satisfies our need for security and significance. In Christ, we discover the who and why of our existence.

The no-nonsense church comprehends man's total dependency upon the power of the Gospel to change hearts, attitudes, and mindsets after the likeness of Christ. The grace of God enables his people to listen with their hearts, as they apply the teachings of our Lord in victory over the prison of the flesh. This victory brings freedom. "The truth shall set you free."[18] In Christ, we acquire freedom from the enslavement of our flesh. In Christ, we are free to believe, to trust, and to celebrate life by giving as God gave to us.[19]

Giving is the divine principle of letting go. God does not need our money, he desires us – our hearts, our devotion, our trust, our dependency upon his power and presence. Sacrificial first-fruit giving involves God's call upon our lives to trust in God. Trust involves the development of self-discipline and self-control. God's love prompts a life of boundaries. Faith enables us to say no to earthly desires, in order to say yes to our hope in Christ.

Failure to exercise trust robs the child of God of peace and joy. Every no-nonsense ministry ought to teach God's people the principal of giving ten percent of first fruits conveyed in the Old Testament. Confusion exists in the church concerning the definition and concepts of tithing. The church ought to not only teach, but also exemplify the concepts embedded in tithing by the way she handles the treasures given by God's people. The issue is not a legal demand, motivated by some fear of retribution from God. Nor is tithing some sort of bribe or "you scratch my back and I'll scratch yours" deal. This is the impression I am left with from listening to some of the high profile preachers.

Tithing presents God's people with the great opportunity to show forth their love for and trust in God. God's mindset on the principles of giving is abundantly clear in the Scriptures. God's expectation that his people bond together, worship together, serve together, "go and tell" together, as well as pool together a generous portion of their financial blessings to sustain the ministry involves the foundational and organizational concepts of the Church.[20] The church has traveled far away from her beginnings described in the book of Acts whereby, "All the believers were one in heart and mind. No one claimed that any of his possessions was his own, but they shared everything they had."[21] "There were no needy persons among them."[22]

God's people can become generous givers if they just believe. Motivated by love and driven by faith, every Christian has been given the freedom from the flesh to be generous. Nothing annoys me more then Christians who use the Gospel of Jesus Christ as an excuse to not tithe. The Gospel is not an excuse for selfishness; the Gospel provides the freedom from selfishness. The Gospel is the answer to sin. The Gospel is the power to the fulfillment of all of God's promises. Those who claim faith and then kick and scream, cry and moan at the challenge to give ten percent are hiding under their refusal to live as free people. They are still enslaved by their own justifications and rationalizations. And the louder they cry the more obvious their refusal to be set free.

Genuine believers find joy in giving. They welcome the challenge, the reminder, the affirmation, and the message of faith. I have heard the moans of parishioners who do not tithe cry, "We are giving till it hurts." What they really mean is that it hurts to give. A new "heart set" is needed. God directs His people, "Set your hearts on things above."[23] "Set your minds on things above, not on earthly things."[24]

God's people use fixed income as an excuse for not tithing. Most everyone has a fixed designated income to depend on, some are just higher then others. Maybe in professions that depend on sale's commissions one's income is adjustable, but a great majority of Americans receive a salary that does not change throughout the year. Fixed income is used in reference to the retiree who lives off of a designated income drawn from social security or investment dividends or some other source. Why is this an excuse to not tithe?

Whatever source generates income presents an opportunity to freely and generously give. The Lord supplies those who trust. He may not supply what we think we need at the time or what we desire in the moment. He may not supply earthly treasures at all. The Lord supplies what is truly needed. He will change even the desires of our hearts to reflect our truest needs.[25] The beauty of God's tithing program is that it calls for a response based on what God has given, not what He has withheld. If the income received is less then an individual needs to survive, then clearly the recipient is dependent upon some kind of benevolent assistance to make ends meet. In that scenario, tithing whatever little income one receives will not make or break the situation.

The freedom to give actually increases when one's income is not securing survival. One is as free as the widow in Jesus' day who did not merely tithed, but gave all that she had. [26] God's people live by faith. The world images generosity as foolish. The reverse is true. "Give and it shall be given to you," the Lord of life declared.[27] The no-nonsense church also stands ready and willing to offer appropriate assistance to families, retired or impoverished. In similar fashion, congregations ought to stand together in helping each other.

God's people can be generous givers if they but give. When my wife was a child her father simply threw her into the water in order to teach her how to swim. She learned to be an excellent swimmer. One does not learn to become an excellent giver by analyzing the possibility to death or by figuring the return on the investment. Nor does one become a generous giver by waiting until he/she can logically afford it. People often pray to receive great riches so that they can be generous. First become generous. Maybe God will give you abundance out of which to give. One becomes an excellent giver by giving. There comes a point when you take the plunge and you swim or drown.

God's people can be generous givers if they but love. When life is motivated by the far-reaching and dynamic change that God's love creates within the heart of a person, then that which seemed impossible takes on a new perspective. God feeds and supplies his people the riches of his grace through the power of his love.

When I journeyed to Montana for a black bear hunt, the miles of burned out forests saddened me. I was amazed that out of the dead wood grew morel mushrooms that scores of people came to pick. Such mushrooms were sold on the open market for $100 per pound. Treasures grow out of that which is lost. God is in the business of bringing life to the dead. He is also in the business of giving abundance to those who have lost it all for His sake. Jesus said, "For whoever wants to save his life will lose it, but whoever loses his life for me will find it. What good will it be for a man if he gains the whole world, yet forfeits his soul? Or what can a man give in exchange for his soul? For the Son of Man is going to come in his Father's glory with His angels, and then he shall reward each person according to what he has done."[28]

God's people are called to let go of their tight grips on the world and trust in God for life. God reveals himself, feeds his people, and equips them for the common good. In response, the child of the Heavenly Father gives a first-fruit tithe, supporting the ministry to which he/she is connected. Additional free-will offerings ought to be given wherever the Spirit opens the eyes and heart to see a need and desire a response.

I am convicted that the firstfruit tithe is best given to the general budget. My perspective is not derived from the law, but from the Spirit of wisdom. In giving to the general operational needs of the local church, God's people are challenged to truly "let go" of their own control by giving money into God's hands to do as he pleases; working through the collective wisdom of his people. When we specifically designate our first-fruit contributions we are apt to manipulate our gifts in the attempt to retain control over them according to our own self-centered agendas and shortsighted vision. The flesh does not want to let go of control. How powerful when God's grace matures us in our dependency upon God, especially in the area of our possessions. Life lived by faith, not by sight, not by man's rational arithmetic, is a life surrendered to the Word of God for guidance and direction.

When God's Spirit awakens our spirit from the dead, he implants his love in our hearts. God's love in us produces the confidence of trust we need to respond with generous hearts. God's faithfulness develops the inner peace that surpasses human understanding and settles us in his care. The flesh remains unsettled. Driven by fear, God's people succumb to the greed and selfishness displayed the world over.

This may be observed in countless life scenarios. We may observe the controlling nature of the flesh in the failure of churches to appropriately, much less generously, compensate their pastors, who are sent by God to keep watch over their souls. Please do not misunderstand. Pastors are not typically resentful. They are joyful in the privilege of serving the Lord.

Most pastors tirelessly make themselves available to those in need. Full time church workers do not expect to make an easy living or to get rich. There are countless other professions that are much more lucrative and require much less education and training. Pastors have a servant heart.

The prosperity of high profile preachers tends to drown out the financial plight of the average church worker. The abusive money scandals of a select few seem to verify that all church workers are looking to get rich off of the contributions given to the church. Paul warns pastor Timothy about false teachers who worm their way into the homes of women as lovers of money. But, the existence of scandalous workers does not provide justification for the church to ignore the needs of the rest.[29]

I have noticed that the average pastor today views his financial situation in a more positive light than in the past. I have also observed this to be largely due to the 2nd income of their spouse, not to the generous compensations of their churches. In today's world, two-income clergy households are more common than not. Churches have even come to expect it. I thank God that I've been compensated as a pastor above the average. However, my compensation is less than it was five years ago, creating quite a financial challenge for a one-income family.

Biblical wisdom never leads a congregation to justify inadequate compensation in order to accomplish the mission. Wisdom may lead the congregation to conclude that doing the right thing requires certain staff to be dismissed. However, simultaneously, doing the right thing may also require adding necessary staff in neglected areas of ministry. Regardless, any paid professional minister should be compensated at least as well as the world compensates comparable professions, inclusive of educational and experience factors. And surely pastors should not be impoverished among those who are not.

Pastors ought to be at least in the same salary bracket as the majority of those served. Pastors are bringing to us God's eternal treasures, and usually are doing so 24/7. God's Word indicates the priceless value placed on such servants when Paul reminds Timothy, "The elders who direct the affairs of the church well are worthy of double honor, especially those whose work is preaching and teaching.

For the Scripture says, 'Do not muzzle the ox while it is treading out the grain,' and 'The worker deserves his wages.'"[30] Paul's reference to a double honor is spoken in the context of compensation that bespeaks the office. Congregations frequently seek to "get by" with as little as possible in remuneration of her workers.

The limited resources of the ministry are real. The identifiable needs are endless. The no-nonsense church prays for discernment in using the limited resources provided. Faith is required as decisions are made in the light of God's Word. Realism often leads God's people to review and opt for less expensive alternatives in making decisions that affect the ministry. Never does wisdom opt for doing the wrong (selfish, greedy, sinful) thing as a means to obtaining a fiscally sound end. Poor compensation of paid servants should not provide an easy cover-up for the poor stewardship of members. The impact of the membership's failure to give generously ought to be directly felt by those responsible. Lock the doors, shut off the heat, and/or cancel events. Congregations need to disengage from enabling the poor stewardship of her members by decisions that impact only the paid servants of the Lord. The no-nonsense church seeks to expose selfishness, while promoting the spirit of generosity.

The uniqueness of working for a volunteer institution, whereby the volunteers served determine the compensation of those who serve them, provides a frustrating scenario for pastors. Other non-profit ministries may have a board of directors who determine the salary level of employees or directors. In many congregations the membership at large retains the authority to make such decisions. This usually means a person can attend a church a few times a year, hardly ever contribute of time, talents or treasures and still cast a vote that determines what the pastor will receive in compensation. I cannot think of a more unjust reality.

Congregational ministry presents a totally unique setting for work. Pastors are often viewed and treated as the C.E.O. of the church with regards to expectations, but seldom in regard to compensation. Though they carry most of the responsibilities that a typical C.E.O. would have in a comparable size corporation, no C.E.O. answers directly to every employee. Nowhere in corporate America does every employee gather together to determine the compensation issues of the C.E.O. Actually, most congregations mimic the small business, rather then the larger corporation. In a small business the owner serves the role of the C.E.O. In what small businesses do the employees determine the compensation issues of the owner?

The church is not a business, but rather a ministry. The principles by which a ministry operates are completely unique. Are members comparable to employees or are they more like customers? Nowhere in corporate America do the customers gather together to determine the expenditure decisions of the business. Businesses do cater to what their customers want in regard to product selection and marketing, but no business caters to their customers in regard to spending the profits.

The pastor is not a C.E.O. or the owner of the church. He is more comparable to other professionals, like a doctor of medicine. There are many similarities. A pastor often spends a comparable number of years in higher educational endeavors. The doctor's rigorous and strenuous work schedule, round the clock on-call responsibilities, is all too familiar to the pastor and his family. Pastors are also in the business of bringing healing to others.

There are, of course, differences. The healing that pastors pray to bring is focused on the soul/spirit and looks beyond the grave to eternity. Even though physicians have work that is quite intense and demanding, unlike pastors, they usually have fellow doctors who will cover their time off. The most striking difference is the doctor's paycheck, which brings relief to the financial concerns and stress of the family.

Maybe the best comparison to a pastor is the psychotherapist or counselor. Pastors surely do their share of counseling. Despite the similarities, I believe it is safe to conclude that no counseling practice gathers together all of the clients to let them decide how much they will be charged and how much the therapist is allowed to take home. On the other hand, the insurance companies are quickly bringing the two professions closer in their nightmares of compensation issues.

Churches often compare the pastor's compensation issues to the factory worker or general laborer, ignoring the level of education or administrative oversight required. The various methods used to arrive at the level of compensation for pastors are enlightening.

Denominations may provide a minimum compensation guideline for congregations, but they seldom stress that such suggestions convey only a beginning point.

Gratuities for weddings and funerals may illustrate the faulty thinking that prevails. A typical gratuity given for multiple counseling sessions, rehearsal, and a wedding service may be $50. When one calls the plumber to fix the basement toilet he wants $60 just to look at it and determine what's wrong. The price goes up from there. The average lawyer charges that much just to have a 30-minute phone conversation. Even the electrician or the service call to repair the broken appliance appears to be valued higher.

A typical rationalization for a congregation's failure to adequately compensate their church workers is to protect them from becoming lovers of money.[31] How that justifies the local congregation in her lack of generous support for those who serve is beyond my comprehension. Shall we also refuse vacation time for servants of God in order to remove any temptation to spend their time doing things that are ungodly?

Amazingly, some pastors believe it to be honorable to join the bandwagon of financial martyrdom by speaking out against higher compensation for church employees. I think such pastors are doing the congregation a grave injustice. I am told that a brother pastor once spoke in an assembly that was making a decision on what level of compensation to offer me. He is quoted as having said, "No pastor deserves to make that much money." What a terrible seed to plant among God's people, a poor example of a generous spirit. The salary under discussion was in line with the church body's minimum salary scale.

A pastor wrote to the congregation I serve, "I have also freely given my opinion that the salaries afforded our pastoral staff are far beyond the amount given pastors in the past." All salaries are beyond those in the past! What was his point? He felt a need to plant the seed that the church over compensates her full time servants. How very tragic! What a great legacy to leave with God's people; "I did my best, Lord, to insure that your people did not overpay your servants."

I've also encountered professionals who seem to delight in inviting the pastor to join them at the country club to which they belong, but who then publicly oppose any pay increase for the pastor. There must exist a need for the pastor to remain dependent, rather than equal, in the social standing. Those who have been blessed with much should not only give beyond the tithe, but also provide a public voice for the plight of others. Jesus declared, "From everyone who has been given much, much will be demanded; and from the one who has been entrusted with much, much more will be asked."[32]

A large congregation once promoted herself to me as a "white collar" church. The interview team must have used that term a dozen times in the interview process. I was driven around to look at local real estate that would have been impossible for me to buy at the salary level they offered. I would have had to live a couple of communities away from the congregation. A church that takes pride in her identity, as "white collar," ought to take pride in raising the bar for excellence in compensation. The much smaller congregation of blue-collar workers that I served at the time compensated me $15,000 more than the proud church offered.

Another congregation recently made the decision to embark upon a multi-million dollar capital campaign to further her ministry goals. Less than a year earlier, this same church reduced the benefit package for all professional staff, including pastors, by no longer paying for the worker's family health coverage. Churches need to get their ducks in order. "Give and it will be given to you. A good measure, pressed down, shaken together and running over, will be poured into your lap. For with the measure you use, it will be measured to you."[33] These profound words of Jesus apply equally to congregations.

Overall, pastors, teachers and other church workers are poorly compensated. This becomes even more obvious when one considers the value of the message that pastors bring to our families. The perplexing absurdity is that the hearts of those who love Jesus Christ determine the pastor's compensation. I believe firmly that God allows many churches to struggle in making ends meet precisely because of their selfish treatment of God's servants. Jesus commanded, "Freely you have received, freely give."[34] Congregations lacking the benevolent spirit are reaping what they have sowed. God says, "Remember this: Whoever sows sparingly will also reap sparingly, and whoever sows generously will also reap generously."[35]

One should not expect the world of nonsense to place a high dollar value on those who provide real service, i.e. teachers, police and fireman. Public servants are grossly underpaid in our society. I am shocked at how little our son is compensated for his willingness to sacrifice his life for the nation, and do so in the Middle East over Christmas away from his family. Our culture's wacky value system absurdly rewards those who entertain us through sports and the media. Astonishingly, the church echoes the world's decisions of injustice. Christians who understand how much God has loved them, without deserving it, should be more concerned with undervaluing, rather than obsessed with over compensating her workers.

The awesome reality is that many are. I have encountered the most generous spirits throughout my ministry. My family has been blessed and encouraged by benevolent hearts. Thank you Lord! Car mechanics, hairdressers, lawyers, doctors, business executives, friends and family have all been moved by God to demonstrate the generosity of God's love. Each one gave the impression that it was not I who owed them, just the reverse. For each I am eternally grateful. I have not forgotten. Our family seeks to pass on the spirit of generosity with others in need.

There are also those congregations who express a generous spirit towards their workers. Not only in direct compensation issues, but also in the provisions of sabbaticals, bonuses, holy land trips, and other gratuities. No-nonsense congregations delight in communicating their gratitude and conveying the spirit of generosity to those who serve them. I know of at least one congregation who takes pride that her pastor is one of the top compensated individuals of the congregation. They intentionally desire their spiritual leader to mingle with the leaders of the community, not only at work, but also in play.

Conversely, most congregations are embedded with enough individuals who complain and moan and groan at the hint of overcompensating their workers that they win the day. They convey an attitude that the pastor should serve them whenever they have a need without expecting to be fairly compensated. Pastors should simply be grateful to serve their needs. The pastor's family should hold the same view. Some members have a chronic need to insure that church workers experience the same negatives as they have had at work. If I have heard once, I've heard a hundred times, "well *my* benefits were cut at work."

Wake up, people of God! The church provides a rare opportunity for the average person to actually have a voice in setting the compensation of someone else. Tragically, the average Christian chooses to exercise this privilege by insuring the golden rule is ignored. Sitting on various nonprofit Boards of Directors my attitude is just the opposite. I am determined that those employed, if at all possible, will not have to experience the same as others. Christ taught, "So in everything, do to others what you would have them do to you, for this sums up the Law and the Prophets."[36]

When we are re-created as new creatures in Christ, our lives enter a new dimension of purpose and meaning. Christ commissions us and redefines us from the beginning of our new birth. In the Spirit, we put to death our self-centered miserable sinful self and rise anew in the regeneration of God's love. This newly appointed significance is exemplified in appropriate stewardship decisions.

The sinful flesh does not entirely disappear, not for now. The old adam continues to plague and haunt our every decision. But, the Spirit of the living God resides in us and enables us to overpower that which is unnatural to the self. In the supernatural dwelling of God, we are redefined, re-identified, re-directed and re-determined. Our mission defines our purpose. We discover life beyond ourselves. Prior to God's awakening we are able to live only by the natural flesh that is incapable of understanding, much less reliance, upon God's Word.[37]

In Christ, we are born anew; to a new life perspective, awareness, and commitment. From this life attitude change, Paul says, "Command those who are rich in this present world not to be arrogant nor to put their hope in wealth, which is so uncertain, but to put their hope in God, who richly provides us with everything for our enjoyment. Command them to be generous and willing to share."[38]

The no-nonsense church models corporately what is expected of members individually. The proverbial "practice what you preach" definitely applies. This means that in the prioritization of resources provided, the no-nonsense church applies the principles of Biblical stewardship to all of her business decisions. The management of the gifts of God's people offered freely to the work of God's Kingdom is understood as belonging to God. These contributions have been entrusted to the decisions of the corporate church for use in service to his name. This is an awesome reality that carries with it an awesome responsibility in service to an awesome God!

The decisions concerning what, when, where and how to use the time, talents and treasures given to the ministry are made prayerfully and carefully. This sobering responsibility requires attentive listening to the Spirit of God. Financial management of God's gifts should never be entered into lightly, but reverently, in the same vein that a man and woman enter into holy wedlock. The focus of responsible stewardship decisions is conveyed in the context of being "in the Word, on the knees, and looking beyond the self." All gifts are utilized for the purpose of fulfilling the in-reach and outreach needs of the mission. The task is clear: to share the living Christ with a dying world. The church will always care about the impoverished, hungry, naked, and outcasts of the world.[39]

The practicalities surrounding the accomplishment of such a sacred trust often becomes overwhelming. Many factors contribute to the limitations that any particular ministry venture encounters. The primary factors contributing to the ongoing frustrations and tension in fulfilling the Great Commission of our Lord are the following:

1. not enough money
2. not enough servants
3. not enough time
4. not enough talents

Notice what is <u>absent</u> in the above list. There are countless ideas and endless identified needs; too many for any one church to fulfill. The core justification for the uniting of congregations under a denominational banner is the need to pool resources together in order to accomplish mission objectives. Even then, the opportunities far outweigh the resources available for the desired response.

And yet, God promises to supply the needs of his people. The promises of God's grace are supplied, not according to God's dependency upon man, but man's dependency upon God. No-nonsense ministries that rely upon God's Word constantly rediscover that his promises never fail. God does not condemn his people for not having the resources needed to do his work. Condemnation is aimed at misusing, abusing and failing to use the gifts of God for his purposes. Nor is there condemnation for having great financial wealth. God's sovereignty determines the reality of a church's resources. In his wisdom God chooses that some of his people are very wealthy, like Abraham, Jacob, Joseph, David and Solomon. The Lord plainly warns his children about the danger of loving money, "Though your riches increase, do not set your heart on them."[40]

The no-nonsense church faithfully conveys this truth of God's Word lest her members fall into the seductive trap of self-destruction. Paul said it this way; "People who want to get rich fall into temptation and a trap and into many foolish and harmful desires that plunge men into ruin and destruction. For the love of money is a root of all kinds of evil. Some people, eager for money, have wandered from the faith and pierced themselves with many griefs."[41]

Judas Iscariot discovered this truth the hard way. So do many congregations. Christians who live on the verge of this very destructive reality sabotage many congregations. One does not have to have money to love money. Many who live in poverty often center their lives on the dream of obtaining wealth. Many would sell their soul to become rich, and do. Many ministries in the name of our Lord sell-out the truth and values, adopting unethical practices, all in the pursuit of increased financial support. What foolish nonsense, deceiving and destroying God's people!

The love of money is a real danger. It stripped Judas of his life in Christ, robbed him of the true riches, and stole from him the peace and joy of eternity. When faith ceased, Judas found that he was bound to the lord of this world, the enemy of Christ, Satan. Will this happen to our churches? The handwriting is on the wall for those who refuse to disengage from the nonsense of materialism. The love of money is one of Satan's most enticing traps. After all, there is not a living soul, or congregation, who does not need money in order to live responsibly in this world. The fact that we are dependent on money makes it the most tempting resource to idolize. If we do not reject the destructive call of wealth to control and consume our every desire and decision, we will end up like Judas.

Recall that just prior to the betrayal, Mary of Bethany lovingly poured very expensive ointment on Jesus' feet. Not coincidently, Judas was the one who protested. Judas made the point that the money would have been better used on behalf of the poor people. Sounds very compassionate. Sounds the same as many of our church members who multiply their poisonous rationalizations as to why the congregation should not better compensate their workers or display a more benevolent spirit towards foreign missions. God clues us in to Judas' real thoughts. God informs us that Judas did not really care about the poor but was a thief and wanted the money for himself.[42] What is the real motivation behind the moans and groans of the church's generosity? By nature we are self-centered and greedy people.

Is the church to which you belong a thief? Is she robbing God by failing to bring in the tithes and offerings? Is she refusing to appropriately support the staff that God has set in place to serve her members? Is she wasting her resources on the trivial, unimportant? Is your congregation engaging in self-centered activities that hinder the accomplishment of her mission?

A few Christians, who complain about every detail of the church's expenditures, do so because of some prior awareness (usually from the media) of a ministry's misappropriation of funds. The integrity of a church's handling of contributions is absolutely essential for the prosperity of the ministry. No-nonsense churches remain alert to the trust afforded her by being transparent in the use of all contributions.

In reality, stealing from God rarely happens by members pilfering the offering plates. The vast majority steals from the church by refusing to give back to God what is his. The real thievery going on in most church settings consists of those who nick pick the expenditures of the church because they do not want to feel the pressure to give more. Others gripe incessantly because they are discontent with their own lot in life. This becomes quite evident when the lack of a generous spirit reaches epidemic proportions and the church has to borrow money to remain afloat.

Robbing God regularly takes place regarding the treasures that never see the bottom of an offering plate. Reminds me of the pointed story about the preacher who announces that he has good and bad news. The good news is that the church has more than enough money to pay her bills; the bad news is that it is still in their pockets. The multitudes of those who claim allegiance to Jesus, but refuse to listen to His teachings on earthly possessions, are mere thieves. In the third chapter of Malachi, God decrees that his people rob him when they withhold tithes and offerings for his work. Everything we own belongs to God. We are but stewards, called to manage God's possessions in accordance with His purposes and plans. To ignore His directives is pure arrogance – claiming rights that were never given. And any church that fails to speak the truth in this regard has succumbed to the nonsense of the world.

As keeper of the money purse, Judas used to help himself, as though the money belonged to him. The love of money conquered him. Money warped Judas' judgment and decisions. Money prevented him from clear thinking. How many churches have muddied the truth by stinking thinking and rationales that condone the selfishness of members? Most likely Judas justified his actions somehow, at least before he threw the 30 pieces of silver at the feet of his employers. Christians excel in their excuses and justifications for withholding their blessings from the hand that delivered them.

Christians who claim to love Jesus give only thoughtless left-overs out of the abundance of God's blessings. These followers of Christ do not just hoard 90% of the bounty that God supplies, but 97% of the first fruits or often even more. Odd how people expect God to be present with His answers when needed, but ignore God otherwise. Selfish takers of God's blessings expect the church to be there with open doors to serve their every need, though they do little, if anything, to insure the doors stay open.

And the amazing truth of God's love is that our gracious God is so far above the petty selfishness of the world that He IS right there with his answers every time we are in need. The no-nonsense church is there as well, representing God, shining his light and love, and freely inviting all to receive with no strings attached. God communicates his answers through the generous lives he has raised up to proclaim his Word. The love and generosity of God is fierce and relentless in piercing the darkness of life.

God's grace warns his people against selling out to the things of this world. For Judas, it seemed to happen a little at a time. When once the church gives way to dishonesty and unfaithfulness, the flesh of her members is armed with the strength of the enemy. When integrity is discarded the church begins to lose sight of right and wrong. The light becomes confused with the dark. Blindness sets in and cripples the membership to respond. Do not give Satan a foothold to blind and deceive the church of Jesus Christ. The no-nonsense church does everything to keep trust in God alive, by being in the Word and on her knees in prayer. Those who trust in the Lord possess the victory over sin, death and the devil. God says, "Call upon me in the day of trouble; I will deliver you, and you will honor me."[43]

The church cannot over emphasize the need to trust in God. "Trust in the Lord with all your heart and lean not on your own understanding; in all your ways acknowledge him, and he will make your paths straight."[44] Time and energy in this frantic world is precious. Money is a necessity in caring for others. The provisions that God gives to the church through volunteers and free-will offerings are essential to carrying out her mission. Let God's people not waste the provisions of God's grace on the love of this world. Let children of the Heavenly Father take care of the Father's business. Let all who trust in God seek the blessings of God in order to be a blessing to others. Jesus sternly warned that we cannot serve both God and money.[45] Let the heart of the church digest this divine reality and communicate the truth to her members.

Hurricane Katrina recently devastated the Gulf coast of our nation. At the time of this writing, recovery efforts are underway to rescue the many people victimized by one of the worst disasters in our nation's history. While the media and politicians engage in arguments and accusations surrounding the government's lack of preparedness, countless Christian organizations and individuals are on the scene. God's people are ready and anxious to open hearts, homes, and pocketbooks in time of need.

The no-nonsense church is love motivated and relationship oriented and consequently exemplifies the generosity of the Lord himself. In the generous exchange of life for death, God gave his life in death that our lives might arise from the dead. God's people live and breathe because of God's generosity of love.

God richly gives Christians all that they need for life eternal. The Lord supplies his children with what they need so that they can rejoice in his presence and celebrate his goodness. The Lord supplies his people with abundance so that they can rejoice in his generosity. God's provisions accentuate our opportunities to give in return. The no-nonsense church gives glory to God by reflecting his generosity to the world. "Bless your church, O Lord, to be a blessing! Bless your people with generous hearts that generosity may spread like a wild fire through your churches."

Digging Deeper into the Word of God

1. Read 2 Corinthians 8:1-7. When the Macedonia church was struggling with finances, what does Paul say happened? What do you think was the source of their joy in the midst of their severe trial? When your church is financially struggling to make ends meet, does she
   a. blame the government?
   b. blame rising costs?
   c. blame debt?
   d. blame the poor stewardship of God's people?

Why do churches tend to avoid holding members accountable for their giving practices? Why do Christians seldom plead for the privilege of giving to others? What words indicate that the Macedonian's spirit of generosity was freely given? What did they give first? How might your church grow in the grace of giving?

2. Read 2 Corinthians 8:8-15. In what way does Paul suggest that a comparison with others is appropriate? What is the only proper motivation for the gifts of God's people? Enthusiasm in the beginning sometimes fizzles out in the end. What does Paul direct in this regard? One of the principles of stewardship is to give according to one's means. What does Paul teach about this?

3. Read 2 Corinthians 9:6-11. The Corinthian church was eager to help. How might one church's enthusiasm stir another congre-

gation to action? Does your congregation exercise the spirit of generosity through their budgetary gifts or are certain ministries grudgingly supported? What percentage of the church's budget supports other ministries?

4. Read 2 Corinthians 9:12-15. In what specific ways does your congregation exemplify cheerfulness in giving? Does your church possess the gift of generosity? In what areas of ministry might your church be resisting a generous spirit? How might your congregation encourage generosity in giving without appearing to "always want money?"

5. Read Matthew 6:25-34. Why do congregations worry so much about finances? How should congregations insure that they are seeking first the kingdom of God? How might the recognition that each day has enough trouble of its own be beneficial to your church?

6. Memorize 2 Corinthians 9:11; "You will be made rich in every way so that you can be generous on every occasion, and through us your generosity will result in thanksgiving to God."

Endnotes

[1] Romans 12:6
[2] Romans 7:15-18
[3] Romans 7:21-24
[4] Ephesians 2:3
[5] Galatians 5:13
[6] Matthew 10:8
[7] Philippians 4:7
[8] Joel 2:12-13
[9] Joel 2:14
[10] Hebrews 13:5
[11] Romans 8:31
[12] Romans 14:8
[13] Matthew 27:5

[14] 1 Timothy 6:10

[15] Luke 12:13-21

[16] Matthew 27:5

[17] Matthew 10:9

[18] John 8:32

[19] Romans 6:22

[20] Study Malachi 3, 2 Corinthians 8 & 9

[21] Acts 4:32

[22] Acts 4:34

[23] Colossians 3:1

[24] Colossians 3:2

[25] Psalm 37:4 (cf. Psalm 20:4)

[26] Luke 21:1-4

[27] Luke 6:38

[28] Matthew 16:25-27

[29] 2 Timothy 3:2-6

[30] 1 Timothy 5:17-18

[31] 1 Timothy 3:3

[32] Luke 12:48

[33] Luke 6:38

[34] Matthew 10:8b

[35] 2 Corinthians 9:6

[36] Matthew 7:12 (the golden rule)

[37] Romans 8:5-8

[38] 1 Timothy 6:18

[39] Matthew 25:31-46

[40] Psalm 62:10

[41] 1 Timothy 6:9-10

[42] John 12:6

[43] Psalm 50:15

[44] Proverbs 3:5-6

[45] Matthew 6:24

Chapter 9 – Spiritually Led
(or "Who Is In Charge of This Mess?")

"Do not be hasty in the laying on of hands,
and do not share in the sin of others. Keep yourself pure."
1 Timothy 5:22

The pastor was a jerk of the first degree. Everything had to go his way. There was no clarity between what the Lord commanded and what he demanded. He was a tyrant. Any respect he solicited was given because of his office, not his person. He was arrogant and rude and saw no point in casual conversation. And yet he served his congregation tirelessly for forty plus years and the majority loved him. Actually, it was more of a hate/love relationship. In those years of his service, the congregation learned to cope. Most members had never known another pastor. This one man formed all pastoral expectations and experiences. Under his leadership, rituals (his rituals) were prioritized and rules (his rules) were enforced. Pity the pastor who followed in his footsteps.

In contrast, the faithful followers of Jesus Christ lead the no-nonsense church. One would assume this to be true, but countless testimonies reveal that the violation of this truth is prevalent in far too many congregations of all denominations. Imperative to the health of the ministry is oversight by professional and lay leaders who are personally grounded in the essential characteristics of the church. Disciples of Christ are centered in Christ, grounded in the Word of the Lord, empowered by the Spirit of God, motivated by

God's love, driven by faith in the Lord, oriented around relation-ships and exemplary in generosity, on a mission to share the Gospel of Jesus. Nothing less will do. Anything else involves the church and her activities in frivolous nonsense.

On the other hand, all across the globe, the course of ministry decisions are determined by the many professional and lay leaders who speak and act from years of fleshly baggage. Volunteer lay leaders who are Biblically illiterate and undisciplined in the way of the Lord are called upon to provide leadership in Christian churches. Leaders who have no clue how or why to pray set the priorities adopted by many congregations. Leaders who refuse to prioritize their blessings after the generosity of God frequently decide how best to utilize the ministry's resources. Leaders who are inept at providing personal testimony to their faith sweep the importance of the spiritual aside in order to emphasize the ritual or the status quo.

Christian congregations pay a heavy price for having promoted leaders who are entrenched in the nonsense of the world. When spiri-tual leaders have adopted the values and embraced the ethics of an unbelieving culture, then the church is in trouble. If the truth were told, the foolishness of unchristian leadership engulfs most mainline denominations of the Christian faith. Any Christian not engaged in Biblical study or an active prayer life, any believer not proactively traveling the journey of faith, and anyone not compelled by God's love to give generously to the work of the Lord is ill-equipped to participate in the decision-making that sets the church's agenda, much less provide leadership over others in the Church of Jesus Christ.

The retention of Christian excellence in the church's leadership is complicated. The Biblical standard is lowered out of fear that the proper and appropriate leadership will not be provided. Sustaining this fear is the acknowledgement that no one is righteous. We all fall short of the glory of God.[1] All of us are indeed poor sinners in need of God's forgiveness. This prompts the church to resist setting a standard that might suggest otherwise.

When the church fails to elevate the Biblical standard for spiri-tual leadership the church does no one any favors. Confusion occurs when we fail to distinguish between forgiveness and qualifications. In Christ, all believers are forgiven, but not all are gifted and qualified for spiritual leadership. The unworthiness of Christians humbles them before a gracious God. Humility is a primary characteristic gracing every God-approved spiritual leader. Humility may be misguided into accepting any forgiven sinner into leadership positions in the church. The reverse should be true. The recognition that no one is worthy should compel the church to insure that only God's Word qualifies an individual for leadership roles in the church.

What should not be tolerated among the leadership of no-nonsense ministries is arrogance and false pride, which results in a refusal to repent of sin. Spiritual leaders are repentant sinners and therefore have as a primary characteristic a humble spirit. Humility is an essential ingredient of genuine faith. The no-nonsense church draws a firm boundary in denying spiritual leadership roles to anyone displaying an attitude of arrogance or a holier-than-thou judgmental behavior. Such an individual is not equipped to spiritually lead others.

Occasionally false humility reveals itself to be a cover up for arrogance. When eyes have been open to discern such pharisaic humility then let there exist God-pleasing confrontation and admonition to the one caught in such sin. Confrontation calls a leader into accountability, verified by a sincere acknowledgement and repentant spirit. No less is expected than a clear and observable change in attitude and behavior for a God-pleasing resolution. No less is to be tolerated among those who would lead others into a mature expression of faith.

The no-nonsense church waits patiently upon the Lord in prayer to send qualified leaders. Rather than operate out of fear, no-nonsense ministries are faith driven. They know that God has promised to supply and they are patient in obedience. God will rise up his servants in due time. Abraham comes to mind. Moses, Joshua, David are familiar spiritual leaders supplied by God. All of the patriarchs and apostles are men chosen by God to guide, admonish and encourage the faithful in their dependency upon God.

What do these Biblical leaders share in common? They each expressed a genuine faith in God and they each became entangled in the sin that enslaved them. They were all repentant sinners. They were all men of humility who placed their hope and confidence in God. Spiritual leaders are not selected because they are without sin. In this moment or that one, all leaders will fail in their attempts to live true to the Word of Christ. Peter succumbed to fear when confronted concerning his relationship to Jesus of Nazareth.

Accountability, admonishments, confession and absolution must prevail first and foremost among the leadership of the church. This serves as a role model for God's people. Those who are not struggling against the flesh are not filled with the Spirit of God. Leaders promoting a Gospel other than the one given in Jesus Christ are removed from leadership roles in the ministry.[2] There can be no tolerance for open and blatant defiance of the truth of Christ. Nor should there be a tolerance for leaders who do not possess a hunger for God's Word. Leaders who willingly choose to remain Biblically immature are dismissed. The integrity of the ministry is at stake.

Confusion between the concept of tolerance and forgiveness disarms the accountability issues of congregations. Tolerance over sin should not be equated with forgiveness of sin. They are the opposites. As noted in Chapter 3, confusion has crept into the fellowship of Christ due largely to a misunderstanding and misapplication of the Biblical concept of judging others. All churches would do well to invest in an in-depth study of God's teaching concerning the godly response to sin and sinners.

In the no-nonsense church, pastors, teachers and other church workers, who themselves are accountable to God and to each other, strive to exemplify the teachings of Scripture in their attitudes, decisions, words and deeds. No-nonsense leaders convey a Biblical vision of servant hood. Whenever the professional church worker ignores this, then most assuredly the lay volunteer will follow suit.

Certification programs in the various church bodies for professional church workers insure that they have received Biblical training and are qualified according to God's Word. Paul provides specific guidelines necessary for the qualifications of bishops. How absurd to place in office a pastor, teacher, or other full time church worker who has not proven to be capable of spiritual leadership.

Equally absurd is the solicitation of lay leaders who are not qualified to be spiritual leaders. This is where much of the ministry's nonsense may be traced. Since the congregation's work is dependent upon volunteers, there exists a great temptation towards soliciting anyone who is willing to serve. Even when congregations refuse to twist arms into service, the spirituality of the one sought is often laid aside and treated as irrelevant.

In soliciting leaders, the church must retain clarity on her mission. Non-profit ministries may share certain principles with the "for profit" organizations, but the ministry is still uniquely that – "a ministry." Churches that seek after leaders with the qualities of success in corporate America, void of spiritual gifts, has proven to be a disaster in the making. Few things produce more nonsense in the ministry than spiritual leaders who are not spiritual.

The nature of a volunteer organization provides additional complexities. Fear that the needed leaders will not be provided may again be identified as the culprit. Is the congregation willing to do God's work according to his timetable and provisions? The church typically concludes, "This is what God wants us to do...so *we* will find a way to do it for him."

The problem of ill-equipped spiritual leaders is difficult to resolve. The demand for qualified leaders is high. One of the greatest absurdities that can be observed in the church's life is the solicitation of so called "spiritual" lay leaders who cannot pray aloud in public or share their faith with another. The pressure to fill positions tempts all of us to accommodate ourselves to the ill-equipped leaders under which we are placed. More than anything this has contributed to the epidemic of nonsense existing in the ministries representing Jesus Christ.

No-nonsense ministries will patiently seek to remain available and equipped by God's grace in order that God may accomplish his work through them. God's people tend to get in a hurry. The church becomes anxious. Ministries measure their success by the things they accomplish in comparison to other churches. Congregations point to their numbers rather than their faith for evidence of victorious ministry. In actuality, faith determines the real success of the church.

The church often becomes so engrossed in fulfilling God's promises for him that she hardly leaves room for God to show up. Man's inadequate works too often overshadow God's faithfulness. Caught up in proving our own faithfulness we easily fail to discover God's faithfulness. Distracted away from dependency upon God's answers we lower our standards of leadership in order to provide the answers to our self-made dilemmas. And God allows such nonsense as we run after our own stuff. Eventually, we tire and burnout, hit brick walls of defeat, and/or succumb to the temptations of the flesh in our failures to embrace the life of faith.

This is the inevitable outcome of ministries not led by the Spirit. Rather than try and grow the ministry ahead of God's provisions, no-nonsense churches enter a posture of being "in the Word, on the knees, and looking beyond the self." This creates receptivity to God's leading. Jesus promises that those who ask would receive, those who seek will find, and those who knock the door will be open. This also applies to the needed leadership.

A better solution, than twisting arms and electing leaders who are not qualified to lead others spiritually, is the decision to reduce the ministry's involvements. Congregations need to "wait upon the Lord" to guide and supply them with the people resources needed to move forward in the ministry opportunities presented. God knows better than his people do what is needed to accomplish his plans. As the church moves carefully and prayerfully down the path of God's will, she is called upon to trust in his provisions and not live beyond her God-given means. The no-nonsense church exercises discernment in all ministry engagements.

Opportunities for ministries are endless. The need for the church's work is ever in our face. The first response to a perceived need ought to be prayer. Waiting for the Lord to supply the church with the appropriate manpower to meet the needs presented is similar to praying for an open door. Waiting upon the Lord does not imply inactivity. Waiting involves intensifying the study of God's Word. Waiting intensifies the time spent on knees in prayer. Waiting involves the challenge extended to all members for self-evaluation. Most likely the needed lay leader is already in the congregation's midst. The Lord fine-tunes and strengthens his people during the time of waiting so that they become more equipped to meet the challenges ahead.

A congregation's ministry vision is commonly shortsighted and overly focused on the short-term opportunities. The Lord has the entire puzzle in sight. Let his children move forward with enthusiastic faith as the Shepherd leads us into greener pastures. Otherwise, we will never get there. Moving forward in the flesh, out of selfishness or fear, or with man's agenda, causes Christians to take too many detours away from the narrow path of God's promised abundant life. Lowering the Biblical standards for spiritual leadership to accomplish the ministry of the Lord will always engage the church in nonsense.

Biblical qualifications for leadership in the church are expounded in Paul's letters to Timothy and Titus and include the following:

> a. Spiritual leaders are worthy of respect as noted by their example in word and deed.

"By their fruit you will recognize them," our Lord informed us in reference to his disciples.[3] Paul instructs those called to be overseers in the church to give themselves wholly to the work of spiritual leadership "so that everyone may see your progress."[4] Leaders by definition set examples by practicing what they teach. Paul tells Timothy, "Watch your life and doctrine closely. Persevere in them."[5] Hypocritical leaders lose their following and rightly so. No-nonsense leaders are repentant sinners whose lifestyles reflect genuine humility and devotion to God. They are leaders who receive admonishment constructively and who never tire in the challenge to cast off the sin that so easily entangles them.[6] People look up to these spiritual leaders as true heroes of the faith.

> b. Spiritual leaders convey a genuine faith and a firm commitment to the responsibilities of the office they hold.

Spiritual leaders live by faith. They refer constantly to the need to trust in Christ. Their lifestyles reveal a dependency upon God for all things. They are faithful in fulfilling the responsibilities of whatever office they hold. Lay leaders who were placed in office because they simply did not say no typically fail to live up to the expectations of the office. Leaders who are clueless to the specific gifts that God has worked in their lives are unlikely to discern the calling of God upon their lives. Those who are unable to appropriately decline the opportunity for service typically find it difficult to resign from office when wisdom demands it. As a result the office limps along with unfulfilled responsibilities while the individual lives with the guilt of not keeping commitments.

Those who elected or appointed ill-equipped leaders should share in the responsibility of having placed them in office. Leadership participation in the "twisted arms," desperate pleadings, and/or guilt trips of volunteer servants is nonsense. A proper evaluation should reveal a volunteer's lack of necessary time and/or talent (gifts and abilities) in fulfilling stated responsibilities. Occasionally, individuals may accept an office only to find that life takes a different direction than anticipated. Discernment is then needed to determine whether the disabling change is permanent or temporary. In Gospel oriented ministries there is surely a value in being flexible. A congregation must work with and around whatever changes are encountered. But, to limp along due simply to irresponsible decision-making is nonsense.

> c. Spiritual leaders are not battling an addiction of alcohol or drugs nor exhibiting a drinking problem or any other out of control type of behavior. They present a clean testimony and the absence of any damaging reputation (i.e. not known for foul language, distasteful jokes, pornography, or any other unscriptural attitudes or behavior). They are self-disciplined.

While Christians vary on their stance towards alcohol, we should all agree that spiritual leaders of the church should not have a drinking or drug problem nor exhibit any behavior casting aspersions on the office or preventing a responsible fulfillment of the office. Christians are to exercise self-control and Christian leaders ought to have been recognized for this fruit of the Spirit prior to being placed in office. The no-nonsense church does not turn a deaf ear or close eyes to members ensnared by sin. I know of a contracted lay evangelist who would visit people while intoxicated. Not to mention the danger to others while driving intoxicated, any testimony expressed was discounted by his behavior. I have known many designated spiritual lay leaders who lacked self-control. I am also aware of church leaders who frequent gentlemen nightclubs and often speak using obscenity. Others are addicted to pornography. Many lay leaders seem to enjoy the reputation of telling "off color" jokes.

All of these ungodly scenarios engage the church in perpetual nonsense. God says, "But among you there must not be even a hint of sexual immorality, or of any kind of impurity, or of greed, because these are improper for God's holy people. Nor should there be obscenity, foolish talk or coarse joking, which are out of place, but rather thanksgiving."[7] Nonsense also involves setting in place spiritual leaders who are out of control with their tongue. Cursing, swearing, telling inappropriate jokes and/or stories, foul language, gossiping and/or slandering are not tolerated in the ministry of Jesus Christ, much less among its leadership. Paul says, "Have nothing to do with the fruitless deeds of darkness, but rather expose them."[8] "Be very careful then, how you live – not as unwise but as wise, making the most of every opportunity, because the days are evil. Therefore do not be foolish, but understand what the Lord's will is. Do not get drunk on wine, which leads to debauchery. Instead, be filled with the Spirit."[9]

No-nonsense leadership in the church is not characterized by any behavior that is forbidden by the Lord. Any lifestyle that is Biblically beyond the boundaries of God's will for his people disqualifies the spiritual leader. Those who choose to obtain unscriptural divorces or to live in sexual relationships outside of holy wedlock are not prepared to lead others in God's way. Forgiveness is not the issue. A person who is known around the community as a rebel rouser or party animal or other such ungodly reputations is Biblically disqualified for spiritual leadership. The Bible conveys clearly that an overseer in the ministry "must have a good reputation with outsiders, so that he will not fall into disgrace and into the devil's trap."[10]

This does not rule out a person who formerly had a sinful reputation, but by God's transforming grace has become known for his integrity as a Christian. Paul, formerly known as Saul the persecutor of Christians, is a shining example of a changed life. God enables us to dump our past sins at the cross and place them completely behind us. In the new birth, we are free to serve God without the hindrance of past sins. There are qualified leaders even though they have formerly been divorced, or struggled with alcoholism or other sinful addictions. The qualified leader in the no-nonsense church has provided witness to a genuine confession of sin and faith in the Redeemer AND his lifestyle confirms his new identity in Christ.

> d. Spiritual leaders are not focused on the things of this world, worldly-minded or materialistic. They provide a good example of stewardship over time, talents, and treasures (as observed by such commitments of service to the Body). Leaders are not lovers of money.

We are never in the position to read the heart. Only God knows the inner motivations and thoughts of man. We are responsible to discern appropriate commitments to the ministry. A person who is clearly a poor steward over his life and possessions is not qualified to lead others spiritually. This does not mean that unqualified individuals do not love the Lord or are incapable of maturing in obedience to the principles of faith. Until God produces the appropriate fruit of faith, a person is not equipped to serve as a spiritual leader.

Spiritual leaders who are "lovers of money" and/or "lovers of pleasure rather than lovers of God" have created great damage in the churches they serve.[11] Paul says, "Since an overseer is entrusted with God's work, he must be blameless – not overbearing, not quick tempered, not given to drunkenness, not violent, not pursuing dishonest gain."[12] When the fruit of those who think "godliness is a means to financial gain" become evident, the no-nonsense church appropriately admonishes.[13]

> e. Spiritual leaders are faithful to the truths of Scripture and able to share their faith with others (i.e. first and foremost observed by one's regular attendance at worship and Bible Study). Pastors are apt to teach.

Biblically illiterate spiritual leaders are misnomers. The primary role of a spiritual leader, that supersedes all other responsibilities, is the testimony to the truth of Scriptures. Spiritual leaders, who are Biblically ignorant, especially involving their area of ministry responsibility, have no place in no-nonsense ministry. All spiritual leaders are life-long students of the Word. An observable regular commitment to the study of the Bible is required of any leader overseeing no-nonsense ministries. Leaders can only testify to what they know to be true. A continual study of God's Word aims at producing maturity in expressing the faith to others. Pastors engage in continual study in order to be prepared to teach the Word.[14] Paul says, "And the Lord's servant must not quarrel; instead, he must be kind to everyone, able to teach, not resentful."[15]

All spiritual leaders do not necessarily possess the spiritual gift of evangelism, but all spiritual leaders welcome the opportunity to share their personal faith in God. Leaders in the church do not shy away from articulating their personal faith in the Lord Jesus Christ. The spiritual leader is not hesitant to express his faith and commitment to the truth. "For God did not give us a spirit of timidity, but a spirit of power, of love and of self-discipline. So do not be ashamed to testify about our Lord."[16]

> f. Spiritual leaders are grounded in the faith through
> time and experience (i.e. not a new Christian).

Spiritual leaders are not newly converted Christians. The army does not take a private right out of basic training and promote him to an officer. Nor should the church. In order for one to apply for officer school in the military one needs an undergraduate college degree. A certain standard of Biblical education is a prerequisite for training no-nonsense officers in the Lord's army.

Paul states that an overseer of the ministry "must not be a recent convert, or he may become conceited and fall under the same judgment as the devil."[17] Members new to a particular congregation also need an opportunity to become acquainted with the unique aspects of a specific ministry location prior to spiritual leadership appointments. The membership also needs an opportunity to give witness to the faith and gifts of the new member. Wooing new converts or members into leadership positions too quickly short circuits the humility needed to sit at the feet of others.

g. Spiritual leaders exhibit godliness at home. Their spouse is not noted for gossip or lack of control of the tongue. Spouses ought to be temperate and trustworthy. Spiritual leadership is not hindered by distraction because of unchecked ungodliness at home.

Godly leaders are not immune to ungodliness at home. The homes of spiritual leaders are made up of sinners as well. It is one thing to fall into temptation and another matter altogether different to live oblivious to the fallen state. Homes that respect the Word of God and exercise the godly discipline of prayer invest in an atmosphere of God's presence. Homes that require the family to worship and engage in Bible study develop sensitivities to any ungodliness that makes its presence known. When the home is motivated by the Gospel of Christ to live according to the principles of faith and love the result is a reproduction of faithful stewards. We are to remember, "If anyone does not know how to manage his own family, how can he take care of God's church?"[18]

Satan finds entrance in the household of God through gossip and slander of one another. James reminds us that a tongue is "a fire, a world of evil among the parts of the body. It corrupts the whole person, sets the whole course of his life on fire, and is itself set on fire by hell."[19] James says that the tongue "is a restless evil, full of deadly poison."[20] He emphatically states, "If anyone considers himself religious and yet does not keep a tight rein on his tongue, he deceives himself and his religion is worthless."[21] The spouses of spiritual leaders are also to be self-controlled. They should engage in speaking the truth and building up the brotherhood of believers rather than tearing it down. Many well-equipped spiritual leaders are to be disqualified for leadership positions simply because their spouses are not to be trusted with the tongue.[22]

To provide ready and easy access to Satan, in attacking the membership of the congregation, is defiant nonsense. Those caught up in habitual tearing down of others with the tongue typically do not acknowledge, much less repent of these sinful violations of love.[23] Offering endless justifications and rationalizations for sins of the tongue, immature Christians become instruments of Satan in the Church of Jesus Christ. Jealousy, bitterness, anger and hatred are typical fruit of the out-of-control tongue.

h. Spiritual leaders are hospitable and gentle.

Paul reminds Timothy of the need to be hospitable.[24] Paul repeats this need to the young pastor Titus.[25] A frequent criticism leveled against a spiritual leader is the observation that the pastor is not a people person. "He does not relate well to others." How insane is that for the public office of ministry? Hospitality is a quality also displayed by no-nonsense volunteers. Paul instructs the Roman Christians, "Share with God's people who are in need. Practice hospitality."[26] Peter instructs "Offer hospitality to one another without grumbling. Each one should use whatever gift he has received to serve others, faithfully administering God's grace in its various forms."[27] John instructs, "We ought therefore to show hospitality to such men so that we may work together for the truth."[28]

Gentleness is a close companion to hospitality. Gentleness is the most effective way to solicit a respectful response. Clerks in retail would do well to consider the necessity of gentleness in working with the public. Solomon concluded, "A gentle answer turns away wrath, but a harsh word stirs up anger."[29] Paul models the gentle spirit of a spiritual leader. He reminds the church at Thessalonica, "we were gentle among you, like a mother caring for her little children. We loved you so much that we were delighted to share with you not only the gospel of God but our lives as well, because you had become so dear to us."[30]

In summary, the no-nonsense church calls upon Biblically qualified spiritual leaders to oversee the congregation's affairs. Endless nonsense has invaded the church's operational procedures because the designated spiritual leaders of the church are relegated to a sideshow responsibility. Regardless of how a particular congregation structures the details of administration, Biblically qualified spiritual leaders ought to oversee the entire life of the congregation at every level.

In the second chapter of Acts, the apostles (whose roles we might compare to today's ordained pastors) are concerned that they protect their focus in Word and prayer ministry. Pastors typically have their hands in too many pots to be effective. They are often overwhelmed and overburdened with the administrative affairs of the congregation.

The Apostles chose seven deacons, who were viewed as Biblically qualified and filled with the Holy Spirit, to oversee the "business" affairs of the church. Today's congregations ought to insist upon leaders who are spiritually equipped with regard to all activities, while insuring that ordained ministers are given the opportunity to focus primarily on Word and prayer ministry. To accomplish this will definitely require a visionary strategic plan.

No-nonsense ministry does require strategic planning. Goals towards staffing the congregation with appropriate spiritual leaders require much prayer and patience. I am convinced that the staffing issues of both professional and lay leaders are a major contributor to a church's success or failure. Not just the right amount of staff, but the properly qualified staff is needed to accomplish the specific calling of ministry.

When setting in place additional professional or volunteer staff positions a congregation should listen attentively to the spiritual leaders already in place. The spiritual leaders should rely heavily upon the thoughts of the pastor. He, more than any, has clarity on what specific gifts are needed from individual staff positions. When a voting assembly of members is responsible to select ministry staff, great reliance should be placed upon the recommendations brought forth by the spiritual leaders. The voters may choose to reject the recommendation, but it would be nonsense to select staff that those in leadership positions have rejected. Professional staff selection should be done with great care and much prayer.

Team ministries require a delicate balance of strengths and abilities that are compatible with other team members. Egos may often interfere with the harmony of a good team. Personal baggage frequently disrupts a team's unity. More is at stake than simply getting along. Pulling one's weight is imperative to the accomplishments of the mission. Burn out is more frequent when one staff member carries too much responsibility. Constant and good communication skills are needed for any team to work harmoniously towards the common good of the whole.

Because full time staff may help to make or break the success of the congregation's mission, selection ought to involve more than a few basic lines of written knowledge about a ministerial candidate. Too much is involved to select staff based on irrelevant or skimpy information. Whatever appropriate way information is gathered on a candidate, i.e. written questionnaires, phone call or face to face interviews, a congregation should first prepare themselves by obtaining a thorough understanding of what is needed by the individual fulfilling a particular ministry staff position.

Beyond the typical expectations of skills, education, and experience, a congregation ought to ascertain what personality type would fit well into the present team. What personality characteristics does the congregation cherish? Those values to which a congregation holds needs to be identified; i.e. integrity, honesty, people person skills, communication or counseling skills, work ethics, and attitudes. Especially those virtues that were weaknesses on the part of former staff ought to be identified.

Various secular profile and performance indicators are available for a congregation to utilize, such as the Meyers Briggs Type Indicator. When available, psychological tests may provide helpful insight into one's personality traits. These tools may serve as excellent resources to formulate a composite picture of a candidate's unique strengths and weaknesses. In addition, there are spiritual gifts inventories that some congregations find quite helpful, especially for soliciting lay leaders.

By no means do no-nonsense ministries skip over, ignore, lay aside or skimp on the Biblical qualifications for spiritual leadership. God lays forth the requirements that are necessary for successful ministry and the church would do well to pay close attention to them. The no-nonsense church is committed to rising up leaders who exemplify the truth of Scriptures in their leadership skills. Paul pleads, "Finally, brothers, we instructed you how to live in order to please God, as in fact you are living. Now we ask you and urge you in the Lord Jesus to do this more and more. For you know what instructions we gave you by the authority of the Lord Jesus."[31] No less is expected of the church's leadership today.

Paul also exemplifies spiritual leadership. He testifies; "We put no stumbling block in anyone's path, so that our ministry will not be discredited. Rather, as servants of God we commend ourselves in every way: in great endurance; in troubles, hardships and distresses; in beatings, imprisonments and riots; in hard work, sleepless nights and hunger; in purity, understanding, patience and kindness; in the Holy Spirit and in sincere love; in truthful speech and in the power of God; with weapons of righteousness in the right hand and in the left; through glory and dishonor, bad report and good report; genuine, yet regarded as imposters, known, yet regarded as unknown; dying, and yet we live on; beaten, and yet not killed; sorrowful, yet always rejoicing; poor, yet making many rich; having nothing, and yet possessing everything."[32]

At the end of everyday, those representing Christ testify, "We have spoken freely to you," we have "opened wide our hearts to you. We are not withholding our affection from you, but you are withholding yours from us. As a fair exchange – I speak as to my children – open wide your hearts also."[33] Leaders in the church demonstrate the faith that expresses itself in the love of Christ.

No-nonsense ministries are indebted to the countless professional and lay leaders who press onward in faith, through thick or thin, in good times and bad. These no-nonsense leaders have not perfected the Christian walk. They are kindred spirits with Paul who said, "Not that I have already obtained all this, or have already been made perfect, but I press on to take hold of that for which Christ Jesus took hold of me. Brothers, I do not consider myself yet to have taken hold of it. But one thing I do: Forgetting what is behind and straining toward what is ahead, I press on toward the goal to win the prize for which God has called me heavenward in Christ Jesus."[34]

Professional church workers, who serve 24/7 in spite of inadequate compensation and often in the face of harsh unjust criticism, ought to receive the highest commendations. Pastors who are always under the gun from somebody, but do not allow that to keep them from testifying to God's love, are priceless. They are the spiritual leaders who exemplify the truth of God's love and forgiveness. They are the ambassadors of the Lord, as though God were making his direct appeal to people through them.

And thank the Lord for volunteer leaders who inspire the flock towards faithfulness by their hard work and dedication. Servants who, year after year, refuse to give up in the face of adversity. They persevere in the fight against the nonsense of this world that threatens God's people. We cannot adequately express our thankfulness for the God-fearing leaders among us. They serve Christ by a consistent demonstration of his Word of truth. They keep before our eyes the name of Jesus by their words and deeds.

No-nonsense servants of God take their work seriously, and so they should. God reminds them through James, "Not many of you should presume to be teachers, my brothers, because you know that we who teach will be judged more strictly."[35] God gave Ezekiel an even harsher warning, "But if the watchman sees the sword coming and does not blow the trumpet to warn the people and the sword comes and takes the life of one of them, that man will be taken away because of his sin, but I will hold the watchman accountable for his blood."[36]

The no-nonsense church ever strives to solicit qualified leaders who faithfully impart the truth of God in word and deed. Spiritual leadership is imperative in order for the church to remain Christ centered, Word grounded, Spirit empowered, love motivated, faith driven, and mission focused. Spirit filled leaders keep the generosity of God vividly before the eyes of people. "Therefore, my dear brothers, stand firm. Let nothing move you. Always give yourselves fully to the work of the Lord, because you know that your labor in the Lord is not in vain."[37]

Digging Deeper into the Word of God

1. Read James 3:1-2. Why does James say that only few should presume to be teachers? In what ways do you think teachers will be judged more strictly? What judgment is James talking about? Why would anyone aspire to be a spiritual leader in the Church of Jesus Christ? What point is James making by pointing out the imperfection of all?

2. Read 1 John 4:1-3. How does John say one can recognize a false prophet? Have you ever known a spiritual leader who abused his authority or office? What was your response? How would you respond differently today? Was his abuse a denial of Christ? Read 2 Peter chapter 2. What additional insights does Peter give in recognizing false teachers?

3. Read Hebrews 13:7-9. In what specific ways does your congregation remember or encourage her spiritual leaders? What does it mean to have hearts strengthened by grace? Read Hebrews 13:17. What kind of obedience is the writer to the Hebrews calling forth from God's people? What is the authority to which God's people are to submit?

4. Read Hebrews 5:11-14. Does your congregation provide ongoing Biblical training for her lay leaders? Is such training required of her spiritual leaders? Why is it absolutely crucial that our spiritual leaders regularly feed upon the Word of God? Read 2 Timothy 3:16-17.

5. Read 2 Timothy 4:1-5. In what ways does your congregation assist the pastor/s in their faithful adherence to the public office of ministry? Does your church provide intentional sabbaticals for her pastors? Are pastors provided adequate professional expenses for study and books? Does your congregation provide continuing education for her professional staff? If not, why not?

6. Memorize James 3:13; "Who is wise and understanding among you? Let him show it by his good life, by deeds done in the humility that comes from wisdom."

Endnotes

[1] Romans 3:10-12, 23
[2] Galatians 1:6-9
[3] Matthew 7:16
[4] 1 Timothy 4:15

[5] 1 Timothy 4:16

[6] Hebrews 12:1

[7] Ephesians 5:3-4

[8] Ephesians 5:11

[9] Ephesians 5:15-18

[10] 1 Timothy 3:7

[11] 2 Timothy 3:2,4 (note the entire chapter)

[12] Titus 1:7

[13] 1 Timothy 6:5

[14] 1 Timothy 3:2

[15] 2 Timothy 2:24

[16] 2 Timothy 1:7-8a

[17] 1 Timothy 3:6

[18] 1 Timothy 3:5

[19] James 3:6

[20] James 3:8b

[21] James 1:26

[22] 1 Timothy 3:11

[23] John 15:12

[24] 1 Timothy 3:2-3

[25] Titus 1:8

[26] Romans 12:13

[27] 1 Peter 4:9-10

[28] 3 John: 8

[29] Proverbs 15:1

[30] 1 Thessalonians 2:7-8

[31] 1 Thessalonians 4:1

[32] 2 Corinthians 6:3-10

[33] 2 Corinthians 6:11-13

[34] Philippians 3:12-14

[35] James 3:1

[36] Ezekiel 33:6 (see verses 1-9; cf. 3:16-21)

[37] 1 Corinthians 15:58

Chapter 10 – Forewarned & Armed
(or "Did I Mention That Enough Is Enough?")

"For our struggle is not against flesh and blood,
but against the rulers, against the authorities,
against the powers of this dark world and against the
spiritual forces of evil in the heavenly realms."
Ephesians 6:12

O ur son, Christopher, is a three-time volunteer in the United States Army. Enlisting in the army's infantry, he has served as an airborne army ranger. Such a journey is quite an accomplishment when one considers what is involved in becoming a squared away "special ops" soldier. In order to be ready for the intense combat assignments given to rangers, they must be fully prepared to engage the enemy with the right equipment and the right understanding of the use of such equipment. Training in this regard is intense, repetitive, and thorough. Their physical safety, as well as the success of their mission, is at stake.

In a very similar fashion, God has forewarned his people of the impending dangers that surround us in this world. In order to protect us from such evils, the Lord has provided the armor needed to withstand the onslaughts of the enemies of the soul. The safety, especially spiritual, of God's people is at stake, as well as the success of the church's mission in which all Christians partake. We are, by God's provisions, to put on the full armor of God.[1] This requires intense, repetitive, and thorough training in the Word of our God.

Though prophecy has its claws more in the past reminders of God's grace and deliverance, the history of God's prophetic revelations is also rooted in proclamations of events to come. God's pattern of predictive proclamations involves preparing people in advance for imminent judgment. We recognize this clearly in the story of Jonah whereby this servant of God was called upon to prophecy the destruction of Nineveh. Prophetic proclamations were a call to repentance and recognition of the one true God.

Satan is on the warpath against God's people. The church that no longer accepts the reality of this hideous foe has already surrendered to his tactics. Churches that remain passive and passionless present the devil with little concern. Churches on fire with passionate love for the Savior are constantly engaged in battle.

God has given clear warnings to his followers of the evil that would come against them. God has identified the source standing behind evil. Peter expressed the reality of Satan's fury against God's people this way, "Be self-controlled and alert. Your enemy the devil prowls around like a roaring lion looking for someone to devour. Resist him, standing firm in the faith, because you know that your brothers throughout the world are undergoing the same kind of sufferings."[2] God describes vividly the battle in which his people are engaged; the weapons needed to stand victorious in this battle, and the final outcome for all that remain faithful.

Sorrow gripped my soul when I learned that the pastor, who ordained me into the ministry and was a long time friend of the family, had come out of the closest, abandoned his wife and children, resigned from his ministry and moved in with his boyfriend. To say that I was shocked is a gross understatement. This pastor had served as my mentor during my college years. Not long after, another pastor friend was caught in a city park soliciting young boys for sex. The devastation wreaked upon both of these pastor's families and congregations is horrendous.

Whatever conclusions we may draw concerning the specific correctness of truth conveyed in books like Frank Peretti's This Present Darkness or Piercing the Darkness, these writings do help to capture a sense of evil's reality in this present world. Scott Peck's book, People of the Lie, likewise, provides his readers with a true sense of how evil operates through individuals. One really needs to look no further than the Holy Word of God in the Bible to understand that the evil one desires the destruction of God's people.

Recently, the national news reported that a woman in Texas cut off the arms of her baby and then sang hymns while the baby died. Unbelievable atrocities abound everywhere. What is behind the insidious evil that prevails in this world? Paul sheds light upon our observations. He clarifies, "For our struggle is not against flesh and blood, but against the rulers, against the authorities, against the powers of this dark world and against the spiritual forces of evil in the heavenly realms."[3]

The church of Jesus Christ does not need to fear the enemy. Christ came so that "by his death he might destroy him who holds the power of death – that is, the devil – and free those who all their lives were held in slavery by their fear of death."[4] Jesus said in reference to his church, "the gates of Hades will not overcome it."[5] Jesus directed, "Be faithful, even to the point of death, and I will give you the crown of life."[6]

James reminds God's people to "Submit yourselves, then, to God. Resist the devil, and he will flee from you."[7] Living in true repentance and faith, believers are protected in Christ. John conveys, "We know that anyone born of God does not continue to sin (willfully or intentionally or defiantly); the One who was born of God keeps him safe, and the evil one does not touch him. We know that we are children of God, and that the whole world is under the control of the evil one."[8]

Though Christians already possess the victory over Satan in Christ, they best know their most dangerous enemy and how to combat victoriously. The enemy seeks engagement. Do we really imagine that Satan presents no threats to the church? He is looking to destroy the church just as he attempted to destroy the Son of God. The revelation of our Lord reveals that Satan was behind the insidious attempt by King Herod to kill the newborn King.[9]

Scripture reveals that in coming to offer a sin-payment for the world, the Son of God was appearing in order "to destroy the devil's work" because Satan was the instigator of sin in the beginning.[10] And when Jesus rose from the dead in victory over sin, death and the devil, "the ancient serpent called the devil or Satan, who leads the whole world astray,"[11] pursued the church and her offspring – "those who obey God's commandments and hold to the testimony of Jesus."[12] Satan is in hot pursuit of the faithful.

The closer we draw near to the end of this veil of tears, the more Satan intensifies his opposition to the followers of Christ. "Woe to the earth and the sea," God says, "because the devil has gone down to you! He is filled with fury, because he knows that his time is short."[13] Whatever timeline and interpretation a church adopts in understanding the vision given to John in the Revelation, the reality of Satan and his fury against God's people is clearly attested to since the fall of man in the Garden of Eden. Satan's enmity against Christ and his church will only grow stronger until God's power and wrath forever removes him from the picture. His eternal condemnation is assured.[14] His total and final defeat has been secured by the death and resurrection of the Lord of lords and King of kings.[15]

In the meantime, God's Word has provided ample warning about the intensions of this archrival. Jesus prayed to the Heavenly Father in regards to his disciples, "My prayer is not that you take them out of the world but that you protect them from the evil one."[16] Though Satan will not destroy the church, he surely tries to render the church powerless and ineffective. And his evil tactics are successful wherever he is permitted an entrance and whenever he is able to establish a foothold. Paul instructs, "In your anger do not sin: do not let the sun go down while you are still angry, and do not give the devil a foothold."[17] Paul further instructs with regards to the Lord's servant, "Those who oppose him, he must gently instruct, in the hope that God will grant them repentance leading them to a knowledge of the truth, and that they will come to their senses and escape from the trap of the devil, who has taken them captive to do his will."[18]

Satan entered one of the disciples and instigated the betrayal of our Lord. Go figure it! The church best figure on the presence of traitorous members, sabotaging the faith and instigating divisions among God's people. In explaining the parable of the weeds, our Lord warned, "The weeds are the sons of the evil one, and the enemy who sows them is the devil."[19] Like infamous Cain, these children of the devil mix with the brothers of the Lord, harboring murderous intentions. Filled with hate and indignation against true believers, these instigators of evil impress their nonsense upon anyone willing to give them an ear.[20]

In teaching the parable of the sower, Jesus revealed, "Some people are like seed along the path, where the word is sown. As soon as they hear it, Satan comes and takes away the word that was sown in them."[21] The church needs to realize that this does not necessarily assure that they leave the congregation. Most likely they remain to fight in order to gain a foothold. Satan takes advantage of whatever opportunity he is given to negatively influence the Body of Christ. Jesus once found it appropriate to rebuke Peter with these words, "Get thee behind me Satan, you are a stumbling block to me."[22] Evil loves power and will grab it whenever possible. In recounting the betrayal of Jesus, Luke reports, "Satan entered Judas."[23]

The church made up of volunteers bent on loving each other is a prime target for those who major in manipulative and controlling personalities. The church may be the only setting that many people are offered the platform of power and influence. The church may also be the only outlet that many people find to release their pent up frustration and anger. The church likewise provides excellent opportunities for those who find it necessary to endlessly role-play their childhood baggage.

The avenues granted Satan to search and destroy in the church seem open ended. Paul revealed to the Corinthians, "To keep me from becoming conceited because these surpassingly great revelations, there was given me a thorn in my flesh, a messenger of Satan, to torment me."[24] Though we do not know with confidence what was the specific thorn, clearly Paul attributed Satan as the instigator of his torment. On the other hand, Paul also confidently spoke of God as sovereign in his oversight. The great promise that Paul conveys in his eighth chapter of the book of Romans is evident in his thorn experience; "And we know that in all things God works for the good of those who love him, who have been called according to his purpose."[25] God allowed the messenger of Satan to torment Paul so that Paul's life would remain wholly dependent upon the grace and power of God.[26]

When I returned home one weekend from college, I slept in a twin bed in the same room as my younger brother. In the middle of the night, I was awakened by my brother's voice yelling, "No, no! Stop it. Stop It!" I turned over to see if he was awake only to observe a hideous spirit figure hovering over his body with hands clasped around my brother's throat. My brother was obviously asleep, engrossed in some sort of nightmare. I commanded the spirit to let my brother alone and leave in the name of the Lord Jesus Christ. Immediately the spirit was gone. There is no doubt in my mind that the spirit was tormenting my brother.

Sometimes God opens our eyes to behold the power of darkness. The gift of discernment is the work of God's Holy Spirit within a believer.[27] I believe that when God opens eyes to behold the presence of demons, one is given a glimpse of their true nature. When I was on a trip to Slovakia, making preparations for an upcoming mission trip, there was a definite irritation in the air. Interestingly, Paul refers to the "ruler of the kingdom of the air, the spirit who is now at work in those who are disobedient."[28]

The dear friend that traveled to Slovakia with me, as well as the wonderful host family who always assisted us, were all on edge. There was a definite tension and uneasiness in the air. Lying in my bed that evening, I was praying and feeling regret for having left home.

I arose from my bed and went to the apartment window to look out. Our apartment was sort of set up on a hill and you could see lights from the city below. Outside of the window, down a ways, was a large tree that kind of stood above the buildings. The branches were bare since the leaves had already fallen. There sitting in the branches was a bird – no it was much too large for any bird. What was it? The appearance was like a huge gorilla with a demonic head and wings. I could see the silhouette quite well in the moonlight. I now knew what was troubling our spirits. The Lord had opened my eyes and revealed the darkness behind the scenes.

On the contrary, when Satan allows a person to see him or his workers of darkness, then the presentation is one of seductive deception. The "father of lies" reveals himself in a light foreign to his real nature. After all, his name reminds us that he is the deceiver. "When he lies, he speaks his native language for he is a liar."[29] Paul says, "Satan himself masquerades as an angel of light."[30] When Satan reveals himself he does so to mislead. A growing enticement among Christian teenagers is the attraction of "white" magic, which is deemed as something good. Witchcraft is often presented as either good or evil. "Good" witches supposedly serve God's will. The church needs to wake up to the evil that is seducing our children away from the truth of God.

Most ministries still confess the reality of Satan and the presence of evil in this sinful world. To deny such reality is Biblically nonsense. However, many churches operate as though evil presents no real danger. The Lord begs to differ. Jesus not only sent his apostles into the world to preach the good news, but he also stated emphatically, "And these signs will accompany those who believe: In my name they will drive out demons."[31] Has the polluted thoughts of the world blinded us to the reality of evil's impact upon our churches?

Other churches seem to create the illusion that the devil may, without consent, take you down the path of hell and destruction. Fear of Satan's power seems to characterize these ministries. Yet, here again the word of God speaks forthrightly and plainly, "Submit yourselves, then, to God. Resist the devil, and he will flee from you."[32] Paul proclaims in confident faith, "For I am convinced that neither death nor life, neither angels nor demons, neither the present nor the future, nor any powers, neither height nor depth, nor anything else in all creation, will be able to separate us from the love of God that is in Christ Jesus our Lord."[33]

Two realities are clearly taught by God's Word in regard to the evil one. Foremost, God's people are secure in God's presence through faith in Jesus Christ and not even Satan himself is able to snatch us out of the hands of our loving Savior. Secondly, Satan is a real enemy of God's people, posing a destructive danger to all believers in Christ.

The Bible consistently warns God's believing community about the number one enemy of the faith. Paul tells Timothy, "The Spirit clearly says that in later times some will abandon the faith and follow deceiving spirits and things taught by demons. Such teachings come through hypocritical liars, whose consciences have been seared as with a hot iron."[34] The church of Jesus Christ needs to intensify her recognition of the enemy's intent. The no-nonsense church prays to close the doors on Satan's intrusions into the Body. Whenever God's people strive against the Spirit of the living Christ a window is opened for the spirit of the evil one to interject his poisonous lies and venomous messages of confusion and deception. Demons are "hell-bent" on providing intentional interference to the call of God upon the hearts of his people.

There should be no question that God's faithful are the primary targets of Satan's onslaughts. He wants to destroy those who trust in God. Believers can be confident that their names are included on Satan's hit list. The combative nature of Satan against those who belong to God engages us in a very real battle between good and evil. Peter instructs, "Resist him, standing firm in the faith."[35]

I suppose Christianity will debate endlessly whether saving faith in Christ that insures eternal security is able to be loss once possessed. The church remains divided on whether faith lost was ever actually faith and whether security in Christ can exist in the absence of faith. Regardless of one's conclusions, the Biblical record brings repeated attention to the warnings given to those who possess faith in Jesus Christ for salvation. Paul says, "So, if you think you are standing firm, be careful that you don't fall!"[36] "Be on your guard; stand firm in the faith; be men of courage; be strong."[37]

The writer of Hebrews says, "If we deliberately keep on sinning after we have received the knowledge of the truth, no sacrifice is left, but only a fearful expectation of judgment and of raging fire that will consume the enemies of God."[38] The most sobering of all warnings is expressed in Hebrews; "It is impossible for those who have once been enlightened, who have tasted the heavenly gift, who have shared in the Holy Spirit, who have tasted the goodness of the Word of God and the powers of the coming age, if they fall away to be brought back to repentance, because to their loss they are crucifying the Son of God all over again and subjecting Him to public disgrace."[39]

The mystery of it all will most likely remain this side of heaven, but God has given us ample warning to be on our guard against the evil that prevails against us. We have the assurance of God's protection and his power to fight evil. We need not fear evil. By the grace given to us in Christ Jesus we continue to effectively battle in the war against the faith.[40] We lift up Christ who is able to bring the church into his victory and present his people covered in the blood of the Lamb.[41]

But, we do need to know our enemy and how to defeat his presence in our lives. We need to recognize those who work on his behalf. We need to be fully equipped to defend the faith once delivered to the saints. We need to put on the full armor of God by which we can stand against the schemes of the evil one. As Paul reminds the church, "For God did not appoint us to suffer wrath but to receive salvation through our Lord Jesus Christ."[42]

Ever watch how a lion stalks his prey on one of those PBS wildlife adventures? A lion is very strategic in executing his hunt. Great care is taken to engender terror in a herd, causing them to stampede. Once on the run the immature, weak, and injured animals begin to be noticed by the keen observation of the lion. The lion increases the pressure until one of the less fortunate of the herd is left behind, unable to keep up with his kinsman. At other times, the lion simply watches for his victim to stray from the herd. Unprotected, the stray finds himself no match for the king of the beast.

Much of the trouble experienced by the church is from the devil, like a lion, keeping God's people on the run. He is watching for that fallout, the individuals who cannot keep up because they have chosen not to participate in the means by which faith matures. Satan also waits in hiding for the stray, that believer who is a loner. Separated from the fellowship of believers while justifying the privatization of faith, the Christian becomes an easy target for the evil one. Faith is always personal, but never private. Those who insist on a private faith express a faulty conviction. "Such 'wisdom' does not come down from heaven but is earthly, unspiritual, of the devil."[43]

To be forewarned is to be armed "so that when the day of evil comes, you may be able to stand your ground, and after you have done everything, to stand."[44] The church, as the Body of Jesus Christ, would do well to apply the concept of the armor of God to herself as a collective whole. Not only does the individual Christian need to be fully dressed in Christ, but the church best put on the armor of light.[45] If the church desires to be "strong in the Lord and in his mighty power" she must be equipped by the Lord's provisions to take her stand against the "devil's schemes."[46] This is not optional equipment. Satan is most definitely scheming against the church.

"Therefore," Paul instructs, "put on the full armor of God."[47] God is calling his people, individually and collectively, to take preventive measures against the advances of the evil one. "Stand firm then, with the belt of truth buckled around your waist."[48] This belt firmly held up the inner garment of the Roman soldier in order that it would not interfere with the outer armor. The analogy calls attention to the necessity of having our inner life (thoughts, heart, soul and spirit) firmed up in the truth of Jesus Christ. The inner life, built on the truth of Christ, will not allow the world of confusion to trip us up or cause us to falter. The church's presentation in this world reflects her member's inner reality. From inside-out God's people take their stand.

The no-nonsense church is grounded in the Word of God. The onslaughts of Satan against her do not throw her into confusion. She is nourished by the solid food of God's truths and is maturing in her faith walk. God declares, "Woe to those who call evil good and good evil, who put darkness for light and light for darkness, who put bitter for sweet and sweet for bitter."[49] Through the heavenly manna the church has trained herself "to distinguish good from evil."[50] She is equipped to "test the spirits to see whether they are from God, because many false prophets have gone out into the world."[51] Peter warned the church about false teachers who would "secretly introduce destructive heresies, even denying the sovereign Lord who bought them."[52]

The second piece of armor listed by Paul is the breastplate of righteousness; the righteousness of Christ that has been transferred to our account.[53] His righteousness has brought us forgiveness of sin that now enables us to stand against the temptations of sin.[54] The power of the Holy Spirit transforms our hearts through faith in Christ. We become the righteous instruments of his presence. "For in the gospel a righteousness from God is revealed, a righteousness that is by faith from first to last, just as it is written: 'The righteous will live by faith.'"[55]

The no-nonsense church owes her existence and identity to the righteousness of Christ. His breastplate protects the heart, formerly contaminated by sin, now cleansed by the blood of the Lamb. The condemnation that threatens the church's extermination because "there is no one righteous, not even one; there is no one who understands, no one who seeks God," is unable to penetrate the breastplate of righteousness."[56] For on this breastplate, written in blood, is the very signature of the world's Savior, God himself. "This righteousness from God comes through faith in Jesus Christ to all who believe. There is no difference, for all have sinned and fall short of the glory of God and are justified freely by his grace through the redemption that came by Christ Jesus."[57] The heart of the Church operates under the protection of her Redeemer and, therefore, the Church stands victoriously against any evil that comes against her. The breastplate of righteousness insures the Church's integrity under the Lordship of Jesus Christ.

The third piece of armor mentioned by Paul is "feet fitted with the readiness that comes form the Gospel of peace."[58] This armor brings to the attention two needs that the church ought to consider in depth. Feet so fitted enable the Body to be surefooted. Anchored firmly on the rock, the church will not stumble. "Feet fitted" proceeds from the Prince of Peace. This insures the church's stability. The Gospel of Christ empowers the church to stand confidently against any troubled waters. No matter how high the torrent, the church will stand without fear of drowning.

The feet fitted with "readiness" reminds the church that she is saved from sin *for service* to the Lord Jesus Christ. Peter calls God's people the chosen "through the sanctifying work of the Spirit for obedience to Jesus Christ."[59] Isaiah said, "Here am I, send me!"[60] The no-nonsense church stands ready; motivated by the love of Jesus Christ that brought her true peace, to go anywhere and everywhere the Lord God sends her. And wherever God sends her she will stand successfully and effectively against the evil one. The Spirit of the living Christ will insure it.

"In addition to all this, take up the shield of faith, with which you can extinguish all the flaming arrows of the evil one."[61] Our faith provides a shield from all that Satan throws our way. With abiding confident trust in God's grace, mercy and power, love and forgiveness, the church is not burned by the lies and monstrosities of Satan or his cohorts. The church can live by faith and extinguish all attempts of the evil one in trying to destroy her, or, the church can play with fire and expect to get burned.

Finally, Paul says, "Take the helmet of salvation and the sword of the Spirit, which is the Word of God."[62] The helmet of salvation refers primarily to the hope of salvation. Paul says, "Do not conform any longer to the pattern of this world, but be transformed by the renewing of your mind."[63] With the helmet of salvation securely fastened on the head, the mind is protected from the secular humanism and philosophies of the world. The helmet provided protection for the head. Without the head, the body cannot survive. Guard your minds with the hope of salvation. Paul says to the church, ""Set your minds on things above, not on earthly things."[64] Scripture says that the unspiritual mind puffs up the arrogant with idle notions. The enemies of the cross set their minds on earthly things.[65]

This brings us in touch with an additional analogy embedded in the concept of the helmet of salvation. The head imagery reminds us that only in the Head of the Body; namely Jesus Christ, is there found the hope of salvation. The Body needs the Head. For the church to wear the helmet of salvation is to set her mind upon Jesus.[66] Otherwise, the church "has lost connection with the head, from whom the whole body, supported and held together by its ligaments and sinews, grows as God causes it to grow."[67]

The helmet of salvation is all about maintaining the hope that "does not disappoint us, because God has poured out his love into our hearts by the Holy Spirit, whom he has given us."[68] Confident hope in Christ guides the church in all that she does. Hope keeps the light turned on. Paul commands Timothy to instruct those who are rich in this world to "put their hope in God, who richly provides us with everything for our enjoyment."[69] "We have this hope as an anchor for the soul, firm and secure."[70] "We have put our hope in the living God, who is the Savior of all men, and especially of those who believe."[71] The helmet of salvation inspires us to endure in our Lord Jesus Christ.[72] Paul refers to this in his letter to the Thessalonica church, "But since we belong to the day, let us be self-controlled, putting on faith and love as a breastplate, and the hope of salvation as a helmet."[73]

The sword of the Spirit is the only offensive weapon in the armor of Christ.[74] With the Word, Jesus battled victoriously all of Satan's temptations in the wilderness. With the Word, Jesus will wage final war against Satan's henchman, the anti-Christ, and once and for all defeat evil.[75] Through the Word, we are able to stand our ground and fight successfully the enemies of our soul. Through the Word, our hope is kept alive. Paul says, "For everything that was written in the past was written to teach us, so that through endurance and the encouragement of the Scriptures we might have hope."[76]

Closely akin to living in the hope of salvation, grounded in the Word of God, is a lifestyle of prayer. Subsequent to the instructions to put on the full armor of God, Paul says, "And pray in the Spirit on all occasions with all kinds of prayers and requests. With this in mind, be alert and always keep on praying for all the saints."[77] Paul tells the church at Rome, "Be joyful in hope, patient in affliction, faithful in prayer."[78] Peter also directs the church, "The end of all things is near. Therefore be clear minded and self-controlled so that you can pray."[79] Prayer is vital to the church's success and effectiveness in battling the evil of this present age. Dressed in the garments of Christ, in full armor, the Church stands ready to do battle, as she lies prostrate before the Lord in prayer.

"In the Word, on the knees, and looking beyond herself," the Church engages the world of nonsense and shines the light of hope. No-nonsense congregations are intruders in the darkness. Believers are called to invade the enemy's territory with the light of Christ. Satan is the lord of this world. Dressed in the garments of Christ, equipped with the armor of light, the children of the Heavenly Father need not fear this invasion.[80] On the other hand, let's not imagine that our intrusion will go unnoticed by the evil one. If the presence of God's people is not unsettling to the enemy, then they have become ineffective. If Christians choose to entangle with the seductive lust or lies of this world, then they are dancing with the devil. He who befriends the world is no friend of God.[81] We have been forewarned and armed.

The revelation of Christ has forewarned God's people of impending danger. Forewarned, the no-nonsense church repents and turns away from ungodliness. Forewarned, she proactively disengages from trivial activities that distract her from the real battle of faith. God's people do everything conceivable, by God's grace and power, to avoid becoming bogged down in nonsense. Too much is at stake. The Gospel of Jesus has provided the armor needed for battle. The Church of Jesus Christ will prevail.[82] The God of peace will soon crush Satan.[83] On that we can depend! The Lord has promised that on his watch the Church shall stand till the end.[84]

Digging Deeper into the Word of God

1. Read Revelation 2:8-11. Who is speaking this message to the church at Smyrna? Why does Jesus say the members are rich? What does he mean by a synagogue of Satan? If Satan was to infiltrate the fellowship of believers to which you belong what are the most likely entry points? When Satan is allowed to test the fellowship of believers, what promise does Christ give?

2. Read 2 Corinthians 11:13-15. How can the church recognize the enemy of the faith if he appears as an angel of light? How can the church recognize Satan's henchmen if they appear as servants of righteousness? What appropriate boundaries can the church put in place to guard against the intrusion of evil in her midst?

3. Read John 17:14-19. What does sanctify mean? In what way does Jesus say his disciples are sanctified in this world? What is the prayer of Christ on behalf of his disciples? What can the followers of Christ expect in this world?

4. Read 1 Corinthians 1:18-27. In what identifiable ways does your community view your congregation as offensive? Read 1 Corinthians 3:18-20. What pressures for the church to conform to the wisdom of this world can you identify? Is your congregation offensive to the lord of this world, Satan? How?

5. Read Romans 8:26-27. What do you think it means that the Holy Spirit is interceding for the children of God? (cf. verse 16) Read Romans chapter 8:28-39. This is one of the greatest chapters in the Bible. Familiarize yourself with its victorious message in Christ. Especially notice verses 1, 5, 9, 15, 18, 28, 31, 35, and 37-38. This would be an excellent chapter to memorize.

6. Memorize Luke 12:32; "Do not be afraid, little flock, for your Father has been pleased to give you the kingdom."

May the God of grace fill our churches
with His joy and peace, as they trust in Christ,
so that they may overflow with hope by the power of the Holy Spirit.
Give all glory to God!

Endnotes

[1] Ephesians 6:11

[2] 1 Peter 5:8

[3] Ephesians 6:12

[4] Hebrews 2:14-15

[5] Matthew 16:18

[6] Revelation 2:10

[7] James 4:7b

[8] 1 John 5:18-19 (cf. Acts 10:38)

[9] Matthew 2:13-18 (cf. Revelation 12:4-5)

[10] 1 John 3:8

[11] Revelation 12:9

[12] Revelation 12:17

[13] Revelation 12:12

[14] Revelation 20:10

[15] Revelation 19:16

[16] John 17:15

[17] Ephesians 4:26-27

[18] 2 Timothy 2:25-26

[19] Matthew 13:39

[20] 1 John 3:12

[21] Mark 4:15 (cf. Luke 8:12)

[22] Matthew 16:23

[23] Luke 22:3

[24] 2 Corinthians 12:7

[25] Romans 8:28

[26] 2 Corinthians 12:9-10

[27] 1 Corinthians 2:14 (cf. 1 Corinthians 12:10)

28 Ephesians 2:2

29 John 8:44

30 2 Corinthians 11:14

31 Mark 16:17 (cf. Mark 3:15; 6:13; Luke 9:1; 10:17)

32 James 4:7

33 Romans 8:38-39

34 1 Timothy 4:1-2

35 1 Peter 5:9a

36 1 Corinthians 10:12

37 1 Corinthians 16:13

38 Hebrews 10:26-27

39 Hebrews 6:4-6

40 1 Timothy 6:12a

41 Jude: 24 (cf. Ephesians 5:25-27)

42 1 Thessalonians 5:9

43 James 3:15

44 Ephesians 6:13

45 Romans 13:12

46 Ephesians 6:10-11

47 Ephesians 6:13

48 Ephesians 6:14

49 Isaiah 5:20

50 Hebrews 5:14

51 1 John 4:1 (see verses 2-6)

52 2 Peter 2:1 (see verses 1-4; cf. 1 Timothy 6:3-5; Matthew 24:24)

53 Ephesians 6:14

54 Romans 12:21

55 Romans 1:17

56 Romans 3:10 (see 3:9-18)

57 Romans 3:22-24

58 Ephesians 6:15

59 1 Peter 1:2 (cf. Ephesians 2:10)

60 Isaiah 6:8

61 Ephesians 6:16

62 Ephesians 6:17

63 Romans 12:2

64 Colossians 3:2

[65] Philippians 3:19

[66] Hebrews 12:2

[67] Colossians 2:18-19

[68] Romans 5:5

[69] 1 Timothy 6:17

[70] Hebrews 6:19

[71] 1 Timothy 4:10

[72] 1 Thessalonians 1:3

[73] 1 Thessalonians 5:8

[74] Ephesians 6:17

[75] Revelation 19:11-16

[76] Romans 15:4

[77] Ephesians 6:18

[78] Romans 12:12

[79] 1 Peter 4:7

[80] Romans 13:12, 14 (cf. Matthew 22:1-14)

[81] 1 John 2:15

[82] Matthew 16:18

[83] Romans 16:20

[84] Revelation 2:7, 11, 17, 26; 3:5, 12, 21

Printed in the United States
47791LVS00005B/136

9 781600 340864